One Step

At A Time

By

Wesley Omoregie

Page Intentionally left blank.

Dedication

This book is dedicated to all those who are walking through the storms of life—those facing pain, addiction, disappointment, rejection, fear, and confusion. To the broken, the weary, the forgotten, and the misunderstood—this is for you.

May these pages remind you that you are not alone, and that no challenge is beyond the reach of God's love. There is hope. There is healing. There is restoration. And there is a Savior—Jesus Christ—who still sets the captives free.

You may feel vulnerable, but in Christ, you are victorious. Take heart. Your story is not over. Victory is possible—one step at a time.

About the Author

Wesley Omoregie—author, speaker, preacher, and counselor—is passionate about helping vulnerable people find hope and healing through Christ. He is the founder of *Step of Jesus Ministry* in California, USA, a faith-based organization dedicated to connecting individuals struggling with drug addiction to free treatment and rehabilitation. This mission is deeply personal for Wesley, born out of the heartbreak of losing his uncle to addiction.

An immigrant based in the United States; Wesley firmly believes that anyone can become anything through Christ. He was raised by his grandfather, a strict Catholic disciplinarian who demanded obedience and church attendance. Wesley was baptized and confirmed in the Catholic faith and knew Jesus from an early age, yet his spiritual journey took a transformative turn in college.

In December 1989, Wesley attended a Pentecostal conference organized by Scripture Union students. A profound encounter with a man of God led him to begin speaking in tongues immediately, marking the beginning of his awareness and experience with the Holy Spirit. Despite this, he kept his Pentecostal faith private during his youth, attending the family Catholic church during holidays and Pentecostal services during school, careful not to let his grandfather know about his new faith expressions.

Wesley fully embraced Pentecostalism after marrying his wife, Rosemary, in 1998. His professional journey began as a high school teacher of Mathematics and Economics, but after a government retrenchment in Nigeria, he entered politics and was elected as a local councilor. He eventually became the Speaker of the Legislative arm in his council. In 2004, Wesley had another life-changing encounter with Christ that called him into full-time ministry.

Today, Wesley balances his roles as a minister, author, and counselor, fueled by his desire to see lives restored by God's grace. He and Rosemary are proud parents to four children—Presley, Daniel, Owen, and Faith—and grandparents to their grandson, Christopher, who continues to inspire their faith journey.

Acknowledgement

First and foremost, I give all glory, honor, and praise to God Almighty—the Author and Finisher of my faith. Without His mercy, grace, and divine guidance, this book would never have come to life. Every word within these pages is a testament to His love, patience, and power to restore and renew.

To the Holy Spirit, my Comforter and constant companion—thank You for Your light, wisdom, and gentle nudges. You have made the message of this book clear, and You continue to guide each step of my journey.

My deepest love and appreciation go to my beloved wife, **Rosemary Omoregie**. Your unwavering support, faithful prayers, and quiet strength have been a constant source of encouragement. You have stood beside me through every season, and I am grateful beyond words.

To my wonderful children—**Presley, Daniel, Owen, and Faith**—thank you for being a continual source of inspiration and joy. Watching you grow in life and in faith strengthens my commitment to walking this journey with God, one step at a time. You are each a blessing beyond measure.

To my grandson, **Christopher**—may your life be filled with God's light, and may you always know the beauty of walking with

Him from an early age. You are a reminder that God's promises span generations.

I am sincerely grateful to **Professor Ugorji** for your thoughtful and meticulous proofreading. Your input refined this work and helped shape it into a message of clarity and truth.

To my **Lecturers at Rhema Bible Training College**, thank you for instilling in me a love for sound doctrine and for equipping me with the tools to rightly divide the Word of truth. Your teaching continues to bear fruit in my ministry and personal walk.

Special thanks to the **Community Church of East Palo Alto, California**, where many of the sermons in this book were first preached. Your faith, hunger for God's Word, and spiritual vibrancy provided fertile ground for these messages to grow. It has been an honor to serve among you.

And to you, dear reader—thank you. Whether you are searching for restoration, clarity, or a new beginning, my prayer is that this book will help you see that with Christ, it is never too late. There is always a way forward—**one step at a time**.

With all my heart,
Wesley Omoregie

Table of Contents

PREFACE

One Step At A Time is borne out of a deep understanding that many are suffering—not merely from physical or emotional hardship, but from a lack of knowledge. Knowledge of the truth that God has already provided an escape route, a way out of pain, confusion, and hopelessness—through the death, burial, and resurrection of Jesus Christ.

Despite being believers, many still struggle to grasp the mystery and fullness of what has been made available to us through our repentance and faith in Jesus Christ as our Lord and Savior. The purpose of this book is to help bridge that gap. It is an invitation to rediscover—or perhaps encounter for the first time—the unending hope and transforming power found in the atonement of Jesus on the cross.

This book was written for those burdened by doubt, weighed down by disappointment, or uncertain about how to begin again after a fall. It is for those whose strength is failing and who wonder if the story of their life can be rewritten. The answer is yes. With Christ, it is never over. In fact, it is often in our weakest moments that He begins His greatest work.

To those who have never truly tasted the beauty and freedom of being a follower of Christ, this book offers you a window into that life—one filled with grace, peace, and purpose beyond understanding.

The content of this book has been developed from a collection of sermons preached over several years. It is not merely theological teaching but a heartfelt effort to encourage you to restart the race of life—with renewed faith, deeper trust, and total dependence on the word of God. His word is a lamp to our feet, a light in our darkest hours, and a source of wisdom for navigating a broken world.

Sprinkled throughout these pages are not only scriptural truths but also glimpses into my personal experiences—real moments that testify to the mercy and faithfulness of God. My hope is that, as you read, you will be encouraged to believe again, to hope again, and to know that no one is ever too far gone for God's love to reach.

Let this book be a guide, a comfort, and a call—to rise again, to walk in the light, and to embrace the identity and destiny that are yours in Christ—one step at a time.

In His grace,
Wesley Omoregie

Chapter 1
A NEW BEGINNING

One of the most challenging years in my life, in the United States of America, was the year 2022. It was a long, interesting ride, and for many of us, it was a turbulent walk. A few may say it was smooth, depending on their successes. But if we look at it holistically or from our congregational perspective or from church leadership, it would be agreed that it was a rough drive.

Every one of us had a bite of the inflation; the price of goods skyrocketed, and the Covid-19 pandemic had lingered throughout the year. So many homes were yet to recover from the loss of a loved one; people were out of jobs in many places around the world, and some businesses had closed due to the new policies of the government to restrict gathering together. Depression had crept into many hearts, and others had become too lonely. Truly, it was tough. And for me, I had struggled through some potholes too and had taken some decisions that came back to hurt me. One example of such a brilliant decision was to go and study for a vocational nursing degree in a private school. I was desperate to open a new path for money-making but did not thoroughly think it through. While I was halfway through the program, I began to feel in my spirit that it was a diversion from my call. My call to be a minister of God is helping to inspire people to enjoy the love of God.

For this reason, I lost over \$20,000, which I had already paid in cash for my school fees. And you can imagine what that may look like when such money came from your spouse and your children! Another painful experience was the sudden resignation of my pastor from our church in June 2022. He left the Church because he was tired and frustrated because of the way he was being treated by the Church Board. He did not inform me about his plans because he knew I would not support his move. He knew I would insist that he should wait on the Lord. The man of God had cried on my shoulder a couple of times and wished there would be peace among the leaders, and I would join him to pray and beg him to be patient. I guess he couldn't handle it anymore.

His departure left a vacuum in my heart because I was only in that church just to shadow him. I came there in response to God's message to go and support him. And I had left my ministry, which had already started in my living room, to join him. I felt so overwhelmed and did not know what to do. Whether to resign as a sign of my loyalty to him! Or to continue standing in his place to ensure that sermons are brought to church every Sunday morning. It was tough for me, and my wife saw my pains and suggested that I leave the church immediately. But I decided to pray about it, but God would not say anything. So, out of reverence to God, I stepped into my master's shoes unprepared. I had to prepare the sermon for the following Sunday to ensure that there was no vacuum created. This situation also led to some useful members leaving the church.

The director of music left; her assistant left; some members in the congregation— which was already highly depleted by the pandemic— also left. But I stayed on in obedience to God and for the continuation of God's work in the Church. That experience has remained in my heart since then, and the pain was so excruciating that I wondered to myself, why did my beloved pastor do this to me?

You see, I am not the only person who experienced difficulties or disappointments that year, before that year, and even up until now. Everyone may not necessarily have my kind of experience. For some, it may have been an illness, a wrong decision, a failure in some expectation, and so on. I am sure there is someone reading my book right now that is familiar with my story. You may have gone through challenges, even much higher than I did, and may have thought of giving up hope. Or you may have fallen into depression out of confusion on what to do. Some may have tried so hard, using every available knowledge and wisdom to solve their problems, to no avail, and may have asked themselves what this is all about. What have I done to deserve all this punishment? You have done nothing wrong, my dear brother or sister; it is life showing you its ugly part, the rule of Satan on earth.

I am glad that you are still alive to read my book right now. I want to let you know that it is proof that there is hope. And for us Christians, we are glad that through it all God did not leave us alone and Jesus was with us all through. Thank God, we made it through, and we are still here. Thank God all these stories are in the past now, and our concern right now should be what to do with our past experience, be it good or bad. And that is why there is a need for a new beginning, a new beginning in Christ Jesus.

Just like the music by Andrea Crouch. "Through it All," if we don't go through challenges or troubles, how do we know that God can solve our problems? If there is no test of our faith, how do we recognize the power of God? How do we know that God is with us?

Every success story is centered around Jesus. He is the New Beginning and the End. Our success starts with God and ends with God.

John 1:1

1 In the beginning was the Word, and the Word was with God, and the Word was God. Verse 2 repeats it: 2. He was with God in the beginning.

Every good thing begins with Jesus. He is in the center of all events. Before creation, He was there with God. He is the Word! Today, He is with us. He is everywhere. He is the Son of God, and He is God.

Without Him, nothing was made. Bring Christ to every decision of your life; bring Him to every plan of your church; bring Him to every plan of your nation; otherwise, you are bound to fail.

Nothing was made without Him. Read John 1:3. 'Through him all things were made; without him nothing was made that has been made.'

I have reflected on several occasions on the name of Jesus. How powerful it is! And I have also thought about the goodness of God. And I imagine His promises and faithfulness: How He promised to be with us at all times and how He promised that if we are willing to turn from our way and ask for His forgiveness, He is more than willing to restore us. The devil is a thief, and the thief cometh not but for to steal, and to kill, and to destroy. Jesus came that we might have life and that we might have it more abundantly. Jesus would cleanse us and remember no more our errors. It is time to start afresh. We cannot keep going in circles. He alone is the way. He alone is the truth, He alone, my brothers and sisters!

I will tell you a story from the Bible. In Exodus 2:11-14, Moses was so eager to solve the problem of his people in slavery in Egypt. He relied on his common sense and on his wisdom to do this. One day, he saw an Egyptian fighting a Jew; he killed the Egyptian and buried him.

He thought he was doing the right thing to solve the problem. But that gesture landed him in more trouble and led to his escape from the king to avoid being killed.

But the same Moses started all over again after forty years in exile because he had had an encounter with God. He saw God in action with the burning bush experience and understood the need to obey God and allow God to take charge. Moses started again on the same mission to free the Israelites, this time around with God at the steering. All he needed was to obey God, and when he did, he became bold enough to face the most powerful king in the world at that time and said to him, Oh King Pharaoh, thus says the Lord. Let my people go.

Have you been facing any pharaoh in your life by yourself? Pharaoh symbolizes an enemy that would not let go of his dominion over your life. He is a strong man. He is the devil. You cannot fight him by yourself. Have you been trying to solve your problem by yourself? Have you been believing in your ability? I am telling you this right now to start all over again. It is time for a new beginning! Allow God to do it for you. As far as I know and understand, your success is determined by your obedience to God. Success is doing what God asks you to do. We were made to serve God, to love Him, and to obey Him. We have no other purpose on earth but to live our lives for the one who paid the price.

Many churches are failing today because the leaders are not listening enough to God's voice. They rely more on their personal ability. They think human. They act human. They do things the human way. Let me tell you again, God is not human. He is a supernatural being. So, we must learn to think supernaturally, act supernaturally, and do supernatural things for things to work in a divine manner.

Go back to your drawing board to plan your life again. This time, allowing God to be in the picture. Only God can enable you to do the impossible. Moses did the impossible because he allowed God into the picture. Whatever you are going through is a phase that will go away. Just refocus on the one who is able to do exceedingly and above all for you.

This should be your New Year's Day! An opportunity to start afresh. An opportunity for a rethink. An opportunity to let God do it for you. Let's allow God to lead us. Amen!

Chapter 2

THE SUPREME LOVE OF GOD

The above parable portrays the supremacy of the love of God for His creation. From the above passage, Jesus gave a true illustration of how important God's love for His children is. It shows the extent a father or a parent can go to protect their own, irrespective of the circumstances or disappointment they may have from that child.

There is an adage in my local dialect that says, 'A bad child can be born but cannot be killed.' No parent would ever want to lose a child, no matter how evil or wicked the child may be. Every parent wants the best for their children.

Jesus demonstrated in this parable to all humanity, and of course including us, that the kingdom of God is accessible to every living being on earth. The kingdom of God is accessible to both the righteous and the sinners. It does not matter how you look or how rich you are. We are all valued alike in the sight of God. And he will go to any length in search of the lost.

This parable of the lost sheep was narrated by two authors in the Bible, Luke and Matthew.

And from what we read in Luke's account, the tax collectors and other sinners were gathering around Jesus. They were eager to be with Him; they wanted to hear from Him. But the Pharisees and scribes were not happy about Jesus' acceptance to mingle with them. They did not like the idea that Jesus would welcome sinners to eat with Him. To them, the tax collectors were not worth being with Christ. As far as they were concerned, such opportunities should be reserved for them. They believe they are righteous and therefore deserve special attention, while other sinners must be prevented from accessing Christ. To them, tax collectors are not to be treated as equals with them. So, Jesus told them the parable to let them know that everyone is valued equally by Him.

Matthew's account started with advice from Jesus to the people not to despise others because they have a guardian angel in heaven who can access God on their behalf. Jesus knew what was in their minds and how they looked scornfully on those they perceived as sinners. That is why he proceeded to tell them the parable of the lost sheep.

The parable of the lost sheep reminds us of what God's purpose on earth is all about. Jesus said the parable to tell the people that He is more interested in the lost. He came to this world to find the lost, the wanderers, and the sinners. Those are His main interests: To find them and to save them: to give them a chance to sit with Him at the dining table as one family. Jesus is more interested in those we call insignificant, those who are homeless, those who are into drugs, those who are not Christians, the unrighteous, the backslider, and all who have gone astray. They are the people God is interested in finding and bringing to safety. They are the lost sheep. Jesus wants to restore them. He wants to bring them back to His light. He wants to make His grace available to them. That is why He came, to give opportunity to all sinners. Every believer is a sheep, and Jesus is the Great Shepherd. The lost sheep are the sinners whom God wants to bring into the ban, to be among His sheep where they originally belong.

Matthew 11:28

"Come to me, all you who are weary and burdened, and I will give you rest.

Our God is in the business of finding lost souls. He wants every one of his creations to be safe.

That is why the shepherd would go to any length to find his lost sheep. He values all his sheep alike. Those who are safe do not need to be found; only those who are lost need to be searched for. The 99 sheep were already in a safe haven. But one sheep was missing and needed to be found. So the shepherd set out for it. That is the way it is with Jesus in His search for lost souls. The righteous are already in a safe place with Christ, but Jesus is still searching for sinners, and this will continue until the end of time. Your commission as a Christian is to join in the search. Join in the search for the lost souls. There are plenty of them missing that need to join the flock.

Luke 10:2

He told them, "The harvest is plentiful, but the workers are few. Ask the Lord of the harvest, therefore, to send out workers into his harvest field.

The truth is that every believer is a laborer; we are His workers, and we are to do the harvesting of souls out there.

Those of us He has found, He commissioned to join in the search. If you are among those He found, join the search. If you are not sure, come to the band and join the flock, the flock of believers; that is where you should be. Are you ready to go and search for lost souls? This is what God wants us to do. That is why He said in His commission in Matthew 28:16-19 to go and make disciples.

Matthew 28:16-19

Then the eleven disciples went to Galilee, to the mountain where Jesus had told them to go. When they saw him, they worshiped him, but some doubted. Then Jesus came to them and said, "All authority in heaven and on earth has been given to me. Therefore, go and make disciples of all nations, baptizing them in the name of the Father and of the Son and of the Holy Spirit, 20 and teaching them to obey everything I have commanded you. And surely I am with you always, to the very end of the age."

Mark 16:15-16

He said to them, "Go into all the world and preach the gospel to all creation. 16 Whoever believes and is baptized will be saved, but whoever does not believe will be condemned. Acts 1:8

But you will receive power when the Holy Spirit comes on you; and you will be my witnesses in Jerusalem, and in all Judea and Samaria, and to the ends of the earth." Without obeying this command, no church can grow. No church can survive, because it is the only command that interests Christ.

Chapter 3
HOPE FROM WITHIN

One of the major characteristics of a good Christian is hope. Hope is simply defined by the English dictionary as a feeling of expectation and desire for certain things to happen. It could be within a time frame or without a known time frame. It is what you expect to happen or what you expect to get. It is hope that keeps a Christian thriving. It is the greatest asset of a believer. Without hope we cannot function as Christians. To me, hope is the switch button for faith. Without hope, faith cannot be activated. In fact, faith and hope cannot work in isolation. They work together.

Every believer acted on hope when their faith in Christ was activated. All of us became Christian with the hope of being with Christ our Creator one day in Heaven, where we shall enjoy eternity with him. We activate our faith to believe in what we hope for. The oil or gas for hope is faith, just like the oil and gas of faith is hope. You cannot embark on a journey of faith without hope. As you put some gas in your car to continue a journey, in the same way you put faith into your hope to continue being hopeful. Sometimes hope can become a great journey that you cannot determine its time of fulfillment. Hope is an intangible thing that you cannot carry with your hands. It is carried with your heart. So also, is faith. They are both from within you.

Hope is like a vision or a revelation, a dream, a goal, or an achievement that you want fulfilled in your life. You carry it in your mind and desire its fulfillment one day. You are passionate about it and want to see it happen. Hope can be in different categories. It can be a wish, it can be an expectation, and it can be sure.

Two types of hope may be distinguished: wishful hope and expectant hope.

A wishful hope does not come to pass in most cases because it is false hope, not backed with faith. But expectant hope has a chance of fulfillment, based on the level of faith and work put into it. It can also be based on the work you have put in. On the other hand, the hope that is sure is guaranteed by your faith in it. There is confidence and assurance that it will surely come to pass. This is the hope based on the word of God. It never fails, and it is sure to happen. For instance, the second coming of Christ is a sure thing to happen because it is based on the word of God. It is God's word, and it must surely come to pass. The word of God is sure because God cannot lie.

"Assured hope" can also qualify as expectant hope because God said it. It is just like when God told Abraham that he would bear a son and that he shall be the father of nations. That was certain, and Abraham waited for it to happen. He hoped for it 25 years before it came to pass. Assured hope is a guaranteed hope because it is always based on the word of God. The Bible records over seven thousand promises of God. So, when you put your hope in any of such promises, it surely comes to pass. Hope is the anchor that keeps you from drifting or backsliding. It keeps you strong and confident.

Revelations that come from God are certain. They are expectations built on the word of God. They can come in several ways and are deeply rooted in your heart like an engraving. Such do not leave you, as they keep resonating.

Those revelations are what we may call a vision, a dream, or an inspiration. These are hopes that God has put in your mind, which can be made to come to pass by you alone.

Have you ever carried an expectation? Have you ever carried hope in your heart? Do you have unfulfilled hope in you? Please know that the fulfillment of that hope depends on your faith. If you have faith in your vision or dream, which has been revealed to you, you do not easily lose hope on it. Your faith keeps your hope alive. Your faith proves that you trust in your hope, and you would not faint in your pursuit. And because faith is propelled by your efforts, you will keep hoping and putting in work until it comes to pass. Hope is certain when it is a Christian hope, because it is strong, trustworthy, and dependable, and it is anchored on the word of God. Just like an anchor holds a ship strong from drifting, so also hope holds a Christian from drifting. However, many hopes, even when revealed to you by God, may fail to come to pass due to your unbelief. When doubt begins to creep in because of the obstacles of life, it becomes very difficult to hold onto hope. That is why we must use the word of God to hold it strong. Let the word of God be the rope you use to tie it to your heart for it to be firm. God has not given us the spirit of fear, but of power and a sound mind. 2 Timothy 1:7

So, we must understand that our vision will always face stormy situations that may discourage us or wear us out to make us lose hope. In every phase of life, whether in the Church, family, or in your personal life, we succeed only when we anchor our hope on the word of God and firmly tie it to our heart like an engraving.

Hope is like a seed planted in the soil. The seed germinates and grows into a plant or tree when it gets adequate water. Water to a plant is like gas to a car and like faith to your hope mixed in the word of God: it makes expectations strong. Faith is the oil or water for your hope. Without faith, hope dies. And without the word of God, faith weakens. As it is that without water your plant will die, so is hope, that even when based on what is revealed by God, it can die if you begin to doubt. You can only keep hope alive when you do not lose faith.

But how do you keep faith in continuous supply? You can only do this by connecting directly to the source of faith. Romans 10:17 tells us that faith comes from hearing the Word. And the word of God is Christ. So, Christ is the source of our faith. Where is Christ? Christ is in you! Colossians 1:27: To them God has chosen to make known among the Gentiles the glorious riches of this mystery, which is Christ in you, the hope of glory. John 14:23: Jesus replied, "Anyone who loves me will obey my teaching. My father will love them, and we will come to them and make our home with them.

Christ is in you. Because you are the temple of God, your hope is within you. It is right there in you. Do not lose your faith; believe in your dream and vision, because God cannot lie. Therefore, you must never forget the rope, which is the word of God. Read your Bible every day to keep your rope strongly fitted in your heart, because you need it to tie your dream or vision or expectations to your heart.

Only you can make your hope be fulfilled. Everything is centered around you and you alone. Phil 4:13 says you can do all things through Christ, who strengthens you.

But the obstacles of life will always try to stop you. That is why your faith and hope hold you up not to give up.

Many times, people hope to achieve certain dreams, but it never happens because of the storms of life. Some would lose a job, some would lose a loved one, some would fall sick, and some would become too stressed out, and they would give up. Some are afraid, and some make

Mistakes, while some are simply deceived or discouraged by friends or relatives or even their loved ones. This is the reality of our world today.

Obstacles are the enemies of hopeful expectations, and what you do with them determines how you succeed. Do not quit your vision because God, who gave it to you, is able to bring it to pass. All you need is to trust the source of your vision and dream, which comes from within you. Christ in you, the hope of glory!

Be firm! Be Bold! and be ready!

In the midst of your failures, move on! In the midst of your disappointments. Move on! In the midst of betrayal, move on! Because Christ in you is the hope of your glory! No matter your obstacles, get up and stand up and fight for your rights. As a child of God, you are entitled to God's gift; you are entitled to God's vision. Do not let the devil take it away from you. Stand up and fight for your rights. Put your hope on Christ, the solid rock. To succeed in your hopes and your dreams, there is always a battle. The battle is not for the weak, so get up and fight for it. Your faith is your gift; hold it strong. Do not lose your grip. Put your hope in Christ alone, and it would be guaranteed to come to pass. I like the hymn that reads:

My hope is built on nothing less.
Than Jesus' blood and righteousness.

I dare not trust the sweetest frame,
But wholly lean on Jesus' name.

On Christ, the solid rock, I stand.

All other ground is sinking sand;
All other ground is sinking sand.

When darkness veils His lovely face,
I rest on His unchanging grace.

In every high and stormy gale,
My anchor holds within the veil.

On Christ, the solid rock, I stand.

All other ground is sinking sand;
All other ground is sinking sand.

His oath, His covenant, His blood,
Support me in the whelming flood.

When all around my soul gives way,
He then is all my hope and stay.

On Christ, the solid rock, I stand.

All other ground is sinking sand;
All other ground is sinking sand.

When He shall come with trumpet sound,
Oh, may I then in Him be found.

Dressed in His righteousness alone,
faultless to stand before the throne.

On Christ, the solid rock, I stand.

All other ground is sinking sand;
All other ground is sinking sand.

Your hope is from within. It is from God. Do not let it fade away. Hold on to it.

Some years ago, I said in one of my sermons that a child first begins to sit and then crawls before he begins to walk. So also, is how your faith works on your hope.

Challenges come, but you surmount them and grow in your faith and become stronger in your hope. Remember how a child will try to stand and fall and then try again to stand until he starts to stand and then run. That is how your faith grows when you fall and then get up again and continue to hope for your expectations. Your faith grows as you mature in Christ until your expectations are fulfilled. Your maturity in Christ comes from feeding on the word.

You are the only one who sees your vision and dream. So, when disappointment comes, you remain hopeful and firm. You dust yourself and move on. When doubt creeps in because of some situations, you erase it again and move on. Do not stop hoping. Do not give up your hope. Remain steadfast and strong, for it is only a phase.

Remember, you may fall, and people may laugh at you. Remember there may be killers of your dreams who will discourage you. You may be embarrassed because of some mistakes. It is only a distraction. Hold onto your hope. Do not give up. Be strong! Be firm and be faithful!

Stand on Christ, the solid rock; all other ground is sinking sand. The reason is because

1.   God will never abandon you.

2.   God's power is greater than any problem.

3.   Every obstacle or challenge leads you closer to your purpose.

When you get tired, remember Abraham's wait for a son; when you faint, remember Joseph in prison. If you become hopeless, remember David's fight with Goliath. All these battles were fought by God himself. He will fight for you, and He will fulfill His promise. Just trust Him.

Chapter 4

THE MOUTHPIECE OF GOD

I am sure that we are all aware that God speaks to us in diverse ways. God can speak to us through His word, through dreams, through visions, and through a servant of God, which can be a pastor, a prophet, or a minister. God can also speak to us through the direct hearing of his voice by the Holy Spirit. Without a doubt, there are numerous ways God can speak to us. However, our human nature and tendencies would not allow many people to hear or see when God is speaking. And for this reason, so many people are falling prey every day to the captivity of the devil and his cohorts. People are falling prey and dying every day in sin because of a lack of attentiveness to God.

Do you know that God is so desperate? Our God is desperate to talk to His children and to warn them about an impending danger. And it is remarkable to see His children refusing to listen or pay attention to what God is telling them.

In the Bible, God made several attempts to warn Balaam not to have anything to do with Balak or the Moabites. But Balaam, in his desperation to gain personal pleasures, would not listen to God's will but continued to seek his personal interest from God. Balaam would have been killed if not for the mercy of God.

Many Christians die out of ignorance because they continue to seek after their own pleasures and personal agendas. They do not calm down to pay attention to what God is saying, and they are unable to discern what God is telling them. Let me give you a preview of what was happening in the above passage. The Israelites have just finished a successful conquest of the Amorites. They defeated Jericho and settled down.

Because their settlement camp was not far from the Moabites, the King of the Moabites became afraid that he would probably be the next victim of the Israelites. He was afraid because he thought he may not be able to fight them. So, he began to think ahead. King Balak understood the ability of a prophet of God and decided to employ one to lay a curse on the Israelites. He knew the efficacy of a curse and knew that if they fought under a curse from the prophet of God, they would lose. So, he went to employ the services of the prophet Balaam to lay a curse on the Israelites. No one excels under a curse, be it an organization, an individual, or a family. Succeeding under a curse is difficult. Well, this will be reserved for another day. I will concentrate on today's message.

Now you must remember that the Israelites are children of God, and God has already commanded Balaam not to do the bidding of Balak. God commanded Balaam not to go with the Moabites, but because of the promises of the king to reward Balaam, he decided to seek God's opinion again. He decided to pressure God to allow him to go.

You can see how so many children of God go after their own will. He wanted God to reconsider. That is how many Christians miss the plan of God. They want to shape their destiny. They do not want the will of God to prevail, and that is why God would allow them to go for their will. That is what we call God's permissive will. In theology, there is a difference between God's will and God's permissive will. God's permissive will is the one you pressure God to do for you, not what God wants for you.

The Bible says in Proverbs 14:12 there is a way that seems right to a man, but in the end, it leads to destruction or death. Balaam pressed on with his permissive will, pushing God to say, "Ok, you can go." And he was bold enough to saddle the donkey and go with the Moabites.

This is the situation with many Christians of today: They go against the will of God to satisfy their own greed and ambition, pursuing their own agenda without seeking the face of God to know what God wants for them. They are easily enticed by their personal desires for money and riches. This is why many Christians fall by the wayside.

God is telling us all today to seek Him first. We must learn how to know what God is saying to us concerning our plans. God's plan for us is a better plan. Jeremiah 29:11. He is always trying to talk to us, but we are not listening enough. It took a donkey to talk to Balaam before he understood the need to focus on God's command. Balaam would have died because he failed to focus on God. He was lucky because God decided to bless the Israelites instead of cursing them, and that is why he lived. The question is how many people would be so lucky or favored this way? Some people would realize their mistake on their dying bed, and others would have gone to jail or fallen ill before they realized. God is always speaking to His own, but how well do we listen? He speaks through his servants; he speaks through our dreams; he speaks through his work and uses people around us to speak to us. How attentive are you?

Sometimes He would use our ordeals and circumstances to speak to us; He would even use other people's tragedies to speak, or the firmament, earthquakes, droughts, and floods to speak; yet people would not listen. How much do we listen? Because people are not listening, there is so much trouble in our society.

God was displeased because Balaam would not hear Him. So, he used an angel to block him by standing on the road. The donkey turned off the road, but Balaam kept forcing it. He beat the donkey harder just to have his way.

Do not be like Balaam; it might be too dangerous. Do not force your will on God. Let His will be done in your life. Balaam was so ignorant that he kept pushing his own will.

Every attempt for the donkey to tell Balaam that there is danger ahead, Balaam would not listen.

Listen to God's message: do not kill the donkey. He is just a messenger. Be critical to know why he is acting strange. Balaam beat the donkey 3 times just to force his personal will.

See what vs 30 says: "Have I been in a habit of doing this to you? Sometimes certain unusual things may happen to you because God is trying to get your attention. He is trying to tell you something. To tell you something very important. Why don't you stop when you experience an unusual situation and ask yourself, is God telling me something? Why don't you pray and ask God to speak to you more clearly?

I will tell you the true story of someone who is very close to me. She was a very devoted Christian while studying law at a university. There was a student who happened to be their Christian group coordinator. The guy was so respected as a pastor by all the group members because they saw him as a very dedicated man of God. One day, the guy proposed to this lady to marry her. And guess what happened? The day the man requested her hand in marriage, they were in a grass field, and as he asked her to marry him, before she responded, a snake from nowhere bit her leg. She was taken to the hospital for treatment.

That experience was unusual, but the lady went ahead to marry the man. She did not recognize that God was warning her not to marry that man. To cut the story short, that marriage became the worst nightmare of her life. The man was only pretending to be a

Christian. He was a dangerous monster. She suffered so much with that man just because she would not listen to God speaking to her.

Sometimes, God talks to us using different means. It could be physical or non-physical. We need to be able to discern in the spirit to understand God. But we cannot discern if we are not close enough to God. How do we get close to God? In truth and in spirit!

Romans 8:14: As many as are led by the spirit, they are the sons of God.

What do you hear God telling you? In His words, what do you hear? In your circumstances, in your troubles, in your challenges, what do you hear? If you listen well, you will hear God. Keep your prayer life active and open your heart to God's voice. Follow the biblical principles to love God with all your heart and to love others as you love yourself. And you will see the antenna to receive will open for you!

Chapter 5
FAITH AND OBEDIENCE

Abraham was tested by God. God gave him an instruction to sacrifice his son.

What this meant was that Abraham would have to kill his only son, Isaac, at the time of the test. This was the son Abraham waited 25 years to get. A loss of that child would mean that Abraham would be left with nothing. No child to inherit from him because Hagai and her son, Ishmael, have been sent away from Abraham's home.

If you read through Chapter 21 of Genesis, you would see the story of what had just happened to Abraham. The same God instructed him to listen to his wife, Sarah, by sending his other son, Ishmael, and the mother, Hagai, away. So, Abraham had just gone through the terrible distress of losing his son, Ishmael. He was recovering from the trauma when God told him to sacrifice Isaac. Isaac was the only child left for him and his only inheritance. A child who has brought laughter to Sarah, his wife.

What do you think was going through Abraham's mind? The instruction from God was pretty straightforward: Kill your son for me! That was heavy!

What would anyone do in these circumstances? Let us think about this for a minute so that we can feel the great burden that Abraham carried on his heart.

Imagine the gravity of this demand on Abraham to understand how much he loved God to have obeyed the instruction. I remember the story of how Balaam tried to persuade God to allow him to go and meet with Balak even though God told him not to go. He insisted on God's approval because of his personal interest, just because of a promise made to him by the king. If God directed any of us to do something that we would never consider doing, how do you think we would respond? Although only very few people hear from God these days, most would not honor His instructions. They hardly believe the message is from God when it contradicts their expectations.

Abraham did not understand why God would want him to sacrifice his only son, but all he knew was to obey God. He did not bother about what Sarah would say or what effect the loss would mean to him and his heritage; all he knew was to obey God. No wonder Abraham is called the father of faith. This was truly a great test of faith.

He did not think twice; he just obeyed. God spoke to him today, and he set out the following day on a three-day journey to sacrifice his son. This is indeed the height of a test and the height of obedience. Abraham passed excellently. He went to the extreme to obey God. This same man waited for God's promise for 25 years. He separated from Lot, his brother's son, on God's instruction. He left Haran, his homeland, on God's instruction. Again, he sent his son, Ishmael, away on God's instruction. For him, it is all about trust and obedience.

Obedience and faith work together. The Bible says without faith you cannot please God. Faith propels action, and the action is obedience. There is a common saying that action speaks louder than voice. How do you respond to God's command?

What will you do to obey God? To what extent will you heed God's voice?

This passage indeed is strong proof that Abraham is the father of faith. He lived a life of obedience to God. His own thoughts or feelings did not matter to him. All he understood was to trust and obey. That is the only way to be happy in the Lord. Just to trust and obey!

However hard the journey may seem, just trust God. However slippery the road may look, just obey God. He is the only key to your true happiness. You are fulfilled in Christ when you have lived a life of obedience. So, you must sit down and ask yourself how you have obeyed God. How have I worshiped Him? How do I improve? What do I need to do better? These are important questions you must ask yourself every day.

Sometimes we do not even know when God is testing our love for him. We do not know when God is testing our obedience to him, because no one understands God's ways. You see how Abraham's test came. It was real to him, and he was willing to obey, even to the extent that he already tied Isaac up, put him on the altar of sacrifice, and even pulled out his knife to kill him before God spoke.

This is the life of every Christian and disciple of God. We are all supposed to trust and obey; that is how we are sure of true happiness in Christ because we never know when God is testing our faith in Him. Our God is a mysterious God; you may not know when he is testing you.

Ecclesiastes 11:5

"As you do not know the path of the wind, or how the body is formed in a mother's womb, so you cannot understand the work of God, the Maker of all things."

Abraham never knew that God was only testing his faith, yet he passed. Who knows how many times he was tested by God? Just like we do not know when God is testing our obedience to Him.

I tell you the truth, trials and tribulations are only a test of our faith. If we continue to trust and obey God, those trials will fade away. Challenges and troubles are proof that our God reigns over all troubles. How else do we know we serve a living God without the trials? These are supposed to improve our relationship with God, draw us nearer to God, and uplift our spirit and prayer life. So, they come to strengthen our faith. No one is beyond trials. But what you do with it determines your level of trust for God.

Do not allow feelings to control you. Let your spirit lead you. Temptation tends to control how we react. We are supposed to respond, not react. When something unusual happens, stop and think before you respond. Ask yourself first, will my response please God? What would Jesus do if He were here? Let your response imitate Christ. This is the way to go.

None of us is perfect or above being tempted. But when we see and understand our limitations and inadequacies, we are able to lean on God and not on our understanding. Proverbs 3:5-6

5. Trust in the LORD with all your heart and lean not on your own understanding; 6 In all your ways submit to him, and he will make your paths straight.

Chapter 6

YOUR NEXT LEVEL

When you form the habit of thanking God for his blessings all the time, you position yourself for greater blessings. When you continue to thank God for His love and mercies everyday, you become a recipient of growth. However, as you thank God everyday, you must make sure that you obey God's command everyday, the command on how to live as entrenched in the Bible. if you obey God's command, He would set you high.

Obedience to God's command guarantees you continuous growth. If you fully obey God, and carefully follow His commands, the Lord your God will set you high above all nations on earth. That is what the word of God says in Deuteronomy. Obedience to

God's voice moves you up from one level of blessing to another level of blessing.

The reason some people or churches never experience growth in their spiritual life is that they do not listen to God's command. Sometimes, they do not even know what God is saying. If you do not know what God is saying, how can you know what to do? When you do not know what to do, how can you take action? This is the root of the troubles of lack of growth in the life of many

Christians today The Bible records in Hosea 4:6 my people are destroyed for lack of knowledge.

Because you have rejected knowledge,

I also reject you as my priests; because you have ignored the law of your God, I also will ignore your children.

The greatest prerequisite for growth from one level to another is knowledge! You can gain knowledge from different sources. From studying, from training, or being told.

The most reliable source of knowledge is divine revelation. Revelation comes from God. Without revelation, you cannot dream big. Without a dream, you cannot see

Vision, and without vision you cannot plan. And without a plan you cannot take action.

Divine knowledge is passed to us through the Spirit of God in us. And the Spirit of God only dwells in God's people; that is, those who are saved by His blood. As Christians, we rely on the Holy Spirit for knowledge. The Holy Spirit is the Person who tells us what we need to know.

John 16:13-15

13 But when he, the Spirit of truth, comes, he will guide you into all the truth. He will not speak on his own; he will speak only what he hears, and he will tell you what is yet to come.

Any church that does not work with a vision or revelation from God finds themselves moving in a circle. And God does not wish that for the body of Christ. His plan for us is a good plan. And I tell you the truth, God is not happy seeing us in one place for so many years. This is not what He desires for His church. Everybody wants growth, no one wants to be in one spot.

Deuteronomy 2:3

"You have made your way around this hill country long enough; now turn north. Then we turned, and took our journey into the wilderness by the way of the Red sea, as the LORD spoke unto me: and we compassed mount Seir many days.

"And the LORD spoke unto me, saying, Ye have compassed this mountain long enough: turn you northward."

It is time to turn around! It is time for your new level. O God reveal to us our new path

Micah 2:10

"Arise ye, and depart; for this is not your rest: because it is polluted, it shall destroy you, even with a sore destruction"

May we not settle for less in Jesus' Name. Amen! We are destined for greatness; we must arise and move on to our next level.

Staying in one spot is dangerous. When you are in a job for several years without a pay rise or a promotion; it is dangerous; you must change your course. Wherever everyone is today is a stepping stone; we are made for signs and wonders. Do not stay in one spot; move up higher and further. Get some training, improve your knowledge and grow. Grow your value.

I remember when I came to the US some years ago. I used to ride on a bus or a train to go to work. After some time, I got a bicycle. But after a while, I changed from bicycle to car. I bought a small car; and after a while, I changed my car for a bigger car

Today, my wife and my children also have their own cars. This is what growth is all about. I was once homeless and had my personal belongings put in the church premises. I once stayed with a friend in California. Today, I am in a bigger house. This is what growth is all about. Growth is a part of God's plan for His people. If we have all experienced growth in our individual lives, we must also experience growth in our spiritual lives. Thus, we ought to experience growth in the body of Christ. If it is not happening, there must be a reason. If we are not seeing the growth, it means we are not catching the revelation. And if we are not catching the revelation, there must be a reason for the clog,

If you are not hearing, stop making excuses, and work on the clog; because it is revelation that can change position not explanation. It is the lack of revelation that is stopping growth.

Revelation breaks the code. There is a force of Light that comes with revelation and darkness cannot comprehend it. You cannot access this light without the word of God. And the word of God must be accompanied with prayers and fasting. When you pray and fast, God reveals the secret code to access His storehouse. Everything you need is in the storehouse. Whether it is about personal growth or spiritual growth or Church growth, it comes from one source, and that is the revelation from God.

You can pray for days asking God why you are not growing or why the Church is not growing and He will tell you: Obey my voice. His voice is His revelation.

God is not a man that will lie.

Let me explain to you clearly how this works. When your WC is clogged, you call a

Plumber; when your car is faulty, you call a mechanic, and when your lights go out due to a burnt cable, you call an electrician. So, it is with life. When your life is not going the way you want, you have to call on God. That is the way this works. Anything that has to do with life or the living, only the Creator can fix it. That is why we are expected to turn to God, no matter how bad it looks. Only God has the solutions to human problems. He knows the beginning and the end. And He has promised to help us. And that is why He sent us a helper in the person of the Holy Spirit. John 14:15

The Holy Spirit is always available to teach us all things. All we need to do is obey His command. We can become whatever we desire to be, but we must be willing to sacrifice what it takes to reach the top. God's plan for us is a good plan. We must be confident, patient and resilient. I pray for you that you shall get to your next level of prosperity in Jesus' name! Amen.

Chapter 7

UNSHAKEABLE FAITH

Some time ago, I preached on the subject of faith consecutively for months. I focused on faith because I discovered that FAITH is the key to God's heart. And for us as Christians to gain access to God, we need the key. The Bible says without faith it is impossible to please God, Hebrews 11:6. And we all know that for a child to receive anything from his father, he must continue to obey his father's instructions and follow his guidance.

So, as children of God, we ought to please God through our obedience and total commitment to His worship. FAITH, therefore, is a total dependence and belief in God for everything. And my deeper understanding of this principle led me to want to know more about FAITH. Faith is formed from a continuous exposure to the word of God. The Bible records that God tested Abraham's faith by asking him to do the unthinkable: sacrifice his son Isaac to God. When you look deeply at the gravity of God's request, you can but wonder how Abraham handled the demand from God. But the swift response of Abraham clearly demonstrated to us that Abraham had an UNSHAKABLE FAITH. He got up early the following day to go about the assignment of God. He did it without worry or fear. He believed in his heart that God, who gave him the child, is able to replace him. Abraham's action shows that he was willing to do anything to keep his relationship with God. And that is what I call unshakeable faith. He trusted God beyond the ordinary. He trusted God beyond the natural. His faith was not of this world; it was of the supernatural.

I am sure Abraham had learned over some years to trust and obey God with all his heart from his previous experiences and encounters. And he was at that level where he was willing to sacrifice all for the love of God. Sometimes I ask myself questions. What am I willing to sacrifice for the love of God? What if God demands of me to do something for him? What will be my response?

From this story, I realized that your faith grows as you obey God's instructions. The level of your obedience determines the measure of your faith. And God provides for you according to your measure of faith. Faith has different sizes and shapes; that of Abraham was mysterious. One of my friends would say in his language, "Igbukeable," meaning unimaginable: too mysterious to fathom and too spiritual to understand. That is why he is called the father of faith.

You see, every believer acts according to their measure of faith, and the measure determines the level. There is a level you get to when you don't think reasonably when God speaks to you. That level is what I call UNSHAKEABLE FAITH: a faith that is not affected by your challenges or obstacles, a faith that is not affected by your human reasoning or human capabilities. You are not moved

42

by what people say or what you see. You are moved only by what God says. It is a state of total obedience. It is crazy.

When you have this kind of faith, you have divine access to God's Throne of Grace, and you have a spiritual ability to draw from the well of the abundance of God.

The abundance of God includes power to access healing, power to access success, and power to access absolute defense, as well as absolute immunity from the arrows of the wicked. In Ephesians 6:16, the Bible recorded that you can extinguish all the flaming arrows of the evil one with faith. UNSHAKEABLE FAITH has no fear at all, because faith is the victory that has overcome the world. 1 John 5:4.

We need to build our faith in God so that we can overcome every circumstance. We need to build our faith to such a level where we fear no more; a level where Esther said, If I die, I die; a level where Moses confronted King Pharaoh and said, Let my people go; a level where people like Jan Huss were willing to be burnt at the stake rather than deny their belief. This is what I call UNSHAKEABLE FAITH.

Somebody may ask, how do we get to this level of faith? Well, we do this by working our way into that nature of Christ, where we can do all things through Christ who strengthens us: Phil 4:13. We need to work our way up to that level where we begin to operate in the spirit as spiritual beings. You cannot please God without faith. Faith is the key to being in the spirit. You begin to function in the spirit when your spirit is in conformity with the Holy Spirit. Romans 8:16 says your spirit bears witness that you are a child of God. Your Faith is a production center. Your faith produces the supernaturalness needed to work in the spirit. We are spirit beings. The Bible says that as many as are led by the spirit, they are the sons of God. Look, all great men that achieved the unthinkable success were led in the spirit. You have to be in the spirit to hear from God. A carnal man receiveth not the things of the spirit. 1 Cor 2:14.

You cannot have unshakeable faith if you do not hear from God. Abraham was always hearing from God. He lived by God's voice, and the things he had seen and done working in obedience to God's voice made it easy for him to be willing to sacrifice his son. His action was a result of a long walk with God. If you hear from God, it is engraved in your heart. It cannot be erased, and what you heard lives with you. That is why the most potent form of hearing from God is Him directly speaking to you. Nothing can erase what God tells you from your heart. When you hear from God directly, your faith grows speedily. Abraham was used to the voice of God: The Bible says, My sheep hear my voice, and I know them, and they follow me.

The word of God builds your faith. If you study the word of God every day, you will come across a message for you. You will feel it's directly for you, and you will receive it as if God is speaking to your heart. I remember when God told me to first seek His kingdom in Matthew 6:33, I heard His voice, and I knew that it was God speaking to me. I tell you the truth: you cannot achieve this height without prayer and fasting. As you pray every day and fast once in a while, you will begin to experience a cleansing of your 'connecting hose' to God. Your antenna will get clearer, and you will hear God speak to you directly. 1 Thessalonians 5:16-17 says we ought to pray regularly to be able to take on the armor of God to withstand all arrows in the days of evil.

Begin to build your faith now so that you can easily tap on it when your faith is needed to carry you through any situation. May God engrave this very important message in your heart so that you can begin to build up faith to the level of being UNSHAKEABLE in times of trouble. Amen!

Chapter 8

THE COMPASSION OF CHRIST

If you read the book of Genesis, Chapter 1, you would find out in Gen. 1:27 that man was created in the image of God.

Gen. 1:27

So, God created mankind in his own image; in the image of God, he created them; male and female he created them.

Theologians always refer to this passage when discussing the relationship between God and man. The Latin word for "The Image of God" is imago dei. The meaning is 'image and likeness of God.' What this simply means is that man possesses the attributes of God. Remember that God breathed life into man after creating him. Gen.

2:7. So, man was created to function like God, his maker. We are capable of creating, capable of reasoning, and capable of communicating. God hears; we hear. God talks and we talk; God feels and we feel. So, we were designed to demonstrate love, just like God does. But the sin of Adam and Eve brought condemnation to man. Therefore, humans came short of the glory of God. However, in His mercy, God gave us another chance through His son, Jesus Christ, who came as a living sacrifice to redeem us and restore us to our original state at creation.

So, you and I are supposed to function as Christ after reconciling with God. And Christ came to live among us, thereby teaching us how we ought to live, using our God-given attributes, as Christ did on earth. These attributes are numerous, but I am only going to talk about Christ's compassion in this passage. Let us read an excerpt from the story of Lazarus, who was raised from the dead:

John 11:25-36

25 Jesus said to her, "I am the resurrection and the life. The one who believes in me will live, even though they die, 26, and whoever lives by believing in me will never die. Do you believe this?" 27 "Yes, Lord," she replied, "I believe that you are the Messiah, the Son of God, who is to come into the world." 28. After she had said this, she went back and called her sister Mary aside. "The teacher is here," she said, "and is asking for you." 29. When Mary heard this, she got up quickly and went to him. 30 Now Jesus had not yet entered the village but was still at the place where Martha had met him. 31 When the Jews who had been with Mary in the house, comforting her, noticed how quickly she got up and went out, they followed her, supposing she was going to the tomb to mourn there. 32 When Mary reached the place where Jesus was and saw him, she fell at his feet and said, "Lord, if you had been here, my brother would not have died." 33 When Jesus saw her weeping, and the Jews who had come along with her also weeping, he was deeply moved in spirit and troubled. 34 "Where have you laid him?" he

asked. "Come and see, Lord," they replied. 35 Jesus wept. 36 Then the Jews said, "See how he loved him!"

The story that we just read demonstrated Christ's love through His compassion for the Lazarus family. He felt the pain of their loss to the extent that He wept. He cried for His friend and was moved with such great compassion that He brought him back to life.

There are few passages in the Bible where Jesus cried or wept. This is to show that He fully demonstrated humanity while on earth. Just like God the Father, the Son had feelings and could feel hurt. And Lazarus' story is one such instance that we just read. Another epistle was during His triumphant entry into Jerusalem, when the people worshiped Him and praised Him. In Luke 19:41-44, the Bible recorded that He wept over Jerusalem, having seen what was to happen to them. Jesus knew that the

The Jerusalem wall would be destroyed, and the great temple would be destroyed too. He saw what was to come upon His people and wept. Another good example was His experience at Mount Olive, the mountain of Gethsemane, when He offered prayers before His crucifixion. In this instance, Jesus was troubled because of the burden of the pain and sorrow He was going to meet at the hands of the Jewish leaders. He knew what He was about to face and wished it would not happen at a point, but knowing the importance of His death, He endured it. The Bible recorded that he sweated blood that night while praying.

Luke 22:41-44

41 He withdrew about a stone's throw beyond them, knelt down, and prayed, 42 "Father, if you are willing, take this cup from me; yet not my will, but yours be done." 43 An angel from heaven appeared to him and strengthened him. 44 And being in anguish, he prayed more earnestly, and his sweat was like drops of blood falling to the ground.

This suffering of Christ was because of His love for mankind. It was due to His compassion for us. He did all this to rescue us from the bondage of death brought by sin. His compassion is unexplainable. It is so much that He willingly paid the ultimate price to save us. He shed his blood to set us free from the wages of sin. Heb 9:22

22 In fact, the law requires that nearly everything be cleansed with blood, and without the shedding of blood there is no forgiveness.

Without His blood there would have been no salvation. The compassion of Christ made this possible. Colossians 1:22 says, 22 But now he has reconciled you by Christ's physical body through death to present you holy in his sight, without blemish and free from accusation— Jesus gave us another chance by his sacrificial death.

Now tell me, what are you willing to give for his love? What are you willing to sacrifice for him?

He gave His life for you; what can you do for him? The knowledge of Jesus' life on earth teaches us how to follow Him. Our major goal is to be like him. As believers, we ought to be like Christ. So, studying about Him and imitating Him help us to be like Him, and one outstanding lifestyle of His is compassion. His compassion is so huge and full of so many blessings. His compassion brings healing; His compassion brings life. His compassion brings forgiveness. His blessings are so good, and it will be unfair to keep them within ourselves alone. That is why He commanded us to share His love: invite others to partake in His feast; bring those who are ignorant of His love to come and enjoy His abundance. Jesus gave a command to His disciples to go out to win souls in order to rescue those who are lost from eternal condemnation.

Mark 16:15

15 He said to them, "Go into all the world and preach the gospel to all creation.

Therefore, one of the major ways for us to show compassion to a dying soul is to win them to Christ. Preach the gospel of the good news that whosoever believes in Jesus as the son of God will be saved. This is supposed to be our contribution to help people who are lost. Jesus already commissioned us, and it is now our turn to commission others and to spread the good news throughout the world to every person who is still ignorant of the truth.

Chapter 9

PLANNING IS WINNING.

Every human being on earth aspires to be a success story. We all want to be at the mountaintop: a place of comfort and excess provision. You cannot get to that height without first imagining yourself in that place. Every one of us has a vision of what we would like to become in the future. Some would like to become doctors, some musicians, some engineers, some would even want to become presidents, and so on and so forth. The list is unending. But surprisingly, statistics have shown that not everybody realizes their vision in their lifetime. As a matter of fact, only 3% realize their dream. The rest will just be a mere wish. And this is because their vision was never backed up with action plans for achieving those goals. One of my mentors once said that planning is winning. just as breathing is living. What that means is that you cannot succeed without a good plan. It is good to have a dream or a vision, but it is better to have a plan.

Planning is the most important tool for success in every facet of life. Without planning, no one can reach a goal. Whatever the goal, social (including family goals), career goals, health goals, financial goals, or even spiritual goals. All goals are achieved through strategic planning. Planning gives value to purpose; without planning, purpose is impotent. A vision that has no plan leads to failure because you cannot get to a destination without a direction. Planning gives you direction. The Bible says, in Habakkuk

2:2, that we should write our vision out and run with it. Without a written vision, it is hard to run with it.

When you write your plan down, it gives you a clear picture of where you are going.

Proverbs 24:3: By wisdom a house is built, and by understanding it is established. This is talking about planning. Every building begins with a plan. A construction without a plan never gets approval. Every organization has an organizational plan, just as every business has a business plan. Church growth is centered around a strategic plan. You plan to fail if you fail to plan. It is as simple as that. Every future must be planned. And the roadmap to your future is contained in your planned goals. Let me tell you the truth: praying without planning is playing without knowing! If you do not plan, you are wasting your time. Success is centered around a circle: purpose, planning, program, and pursuit.

You set out your goals, you plan your strategies, you plan your programs, and you pursue your goals. This is how you get results anywhere in the world. Many churches and many people have been failing for years because of a lack of planning. So if you are reading this book and still do not have a written plan, you are still playing. You better begin to write your plan now.

What is planning? Planning is a design of a step-by-step approach to accomplish a set of goals. It is a process of action to fulfill a dream. You must sit down to plan your goals.

This is very critical to succeeding. Success is not by mistake; it is by sound planning. Planning relieves you of tension.

To set great goals, you need some important ingredients. Every enterprise is built by wise planning. And wise planning must articulate the steps to take into the goals. You must be knowledgeable to plan, and you must plan according to your knowledge or capacity. There is a limit to every man's knowledge: Proverbs 23:7: As a man thinketh, so he is… That is why it is wise to continue to develop your knowledge through studying and reading books. You need management skills to grow a church. You need management skills to manage your marriage, so you also need management skills to manage your life, your relationship, and your vision. Your managerial skill determines how far you can go. If you do not have one, you can hire one. That is what every great organization is doing around the world. Ideas rule the world.

Search for great ideas.

There are three important things you do when you set goals.

1. Set a definite goal. Be specific, clear, and concise.
2. Decide on a deadline. Write down when you must achieve the set goals. Put in a timeline.

3. Run with your vision. Put in an action program and pursue it. That gives you the drive to act on it.

There is no doubt it is hard or not easy. That is why only a few people succeed. But a great plan requires strategic reasoning. Thinking and reasoning must be logical, rational, analytical, and sound. Above all, never be afraid of your vision, no matter how big it is. Believe that the God that gave you the vision is able to make it happen.

Vision is a revelation, but your plans come from critical thinking. You cannot work by borrowed thoughts; you must create your own plan; you must use your brain.

Prayer only enhances the quality of your plans. Spirituality is not against reasoning. Open your inner mind so that God can give you revelations and bring those revelations to bear through critical thinking, and the result will be a great success. Finally, please remember, you will do the planting, and God will water it for you. The buck stops with you.

Chapter 10

GRATITUDE

During festive periods in America, people always give gifts to their loved ones and to friends. Some are postcards; some are simple text messages, while others are food baskets or turkey. This is mostly predominant during Thanksgiving. Shops even give out so many items for cheaper prices. I also managed to give out turkey to some families in 2022. It felt good to be an instrument of giving to others. It was always nice to see people happy everywhere because of the holidays.

As an immigrant in America, I wondered so much about the reason for the Thanksgiving celebration, which appeared to be the most widely celebrated by Americans. So, I had to do a little research about the Thanksgiving celebration, and I found out that it was a celebration that started in 1621. The pilgrims held a harvest feast at Plymouth Plantation in Massachusetts. They were thanking God for a bountiful harvest that year. This was because they had been through a year-long shortage of food, and people died of illnesses during this period until they got knowledge of how to plant corn to get a good harvest. Thereafter, in 1621, and behold, that year they had a great harvest. They were so happy because it turned their situation of lack of food around.

Because of the prayers that were made, they believed God answered prayers. The celebration went on for 3 days. It was a symbolic occasion to the extent that it became their yearly thing until it became recognized as a holiday by Congress on 28 October.

1789. And on December 26, 1941, President Roosevelt signed a resolution to make every 4th Thursday of December a national Thanksgiving Day. The story was so fascinating to me, and I told myself, These people surely understood how to give glory to God in those days.

You see, in all this story, there is one thing that resonates within me. Thanksgiving started as a celebration of appreciation of God's favor. It was all about gratitude.

Shout for joy to the Lord, all the earth. Worship the Lord with gladness; come before him with joyful songs. Know that the Lord is God.

It is he who made us, and we are his; we are his people, the sheep of his pasture. Enter his gates with thanksgiving and his courts with praise; give thanks to him and praise his name. For the Lord is good, and his love endures forever; his faithfulness continues through all generations. Amen!

Thanksgiving is all about gratitude to God for providing, providing especially when there was a great lack. Gratitude is actually about saying thank you: thank you for helping out. It is about saying, I recognized your helping me to solve a problem that I could not solve.

Thank you for standing in for me.

This reminds me of the fact that every individual needs help at some point in their life. But for some unknown reason, we tend to forget when we are helped within a short period. That is why I became very interested to talk about gratitude today. Imagine an event that happened in 1621 still being celebrated today to the extent that it is now a national holiday. It is amazing!

In Psalm 100, King David was saying that gratitude to God should not only be a simple thank you but also a recognition of the value of God in our lives as we thank Him. King David stressed for everyone to shout for joy to the Lord. Worship the Lord with gladness.

Come before Him with joyful songs, because it is not a thing to be quiet about. Praise His holy name and sing joyful songs.

Let the world know you are happy. Let them know that something good has happened to you. That is the beauty of giving thanks to God. You are excited; you jubilate and sing for joy. That is what Thanksgiving is all about: an open appreciation of the favor of God in our lives.

Sometimes, we do not take enough time to dwell on the goodness of God. We tend to forget so easily all the things God has done for us. Even when we receive help from other people, we do not remember beyond the point when we say thank you. When we are in need of help, we go to any length to beg for it. We pray every day; we send prayer requests to the church, and we go to church every day. The moment God answers our prayers; we begin to give excuses for not being able to come to church. When the weather is too cold, we stay at home; when we feel tired, we stay at home. When we have a visitor, we stay at home. We avoid church for every little reason. It does not feel like we were the same people crying to God to help us. God suddenly becomes a stranger.

In Luke 17:11-19, you see the story of the ten lepers who were healed of leprosy by Jesus Christ on His way to Jerusalem. While Jesus walked past them, they screamed for help from a distance. They were desperate for attention because they were in a big mess. They could not even get near to people because of their situation. It was bad. But the moment they received their healing, only one came back to show gratitude. Only one came to say thank you. Even Jesus asked him about the rest of the nine men. Can you imagine only 10% came? 90% of those who got help never came to say thank you.

Because they forgot where they were before the healing. This is the situation with our world today. It is even worse because people forget so easily when things are bad.

Some people are like those lepers. They forget when things were so bad. So easily! They forgot when they were having sleepless nights begging God for help. They forget when they used to struggle to feed. They forget when they had no job. They forget when things were not so juicy. They do not remember anymore. I am sure if you think about your life, you would remember there was a time when it was not so sweet. You would remember when you asked God to come to your rescue. And He came to your rescue. He answered your prayers. But how do you show your appreciation today? Some of us may have had somebody help them in life before, maybe several years ago. But today, they would not even remember if such people exist.

Gratitude must not be a period like our Thanksgiving period. But at all times, we must always remember that there is always something to be grateful about: something that God did for you. It can be through somebody or by divine help; every day we must remember and say, Thank you, Lord. Sometimes we need to sit down very quietly and meditate and remember anyone in our lives that has made a remarkable contribution or helped to affect our lives in a good way. We must pick up our phone to say, I remember what you did. Thank you.

A couple of years ago, I was on my Facebook page, and someone called me with a Facebook call. I did not remember the face, but I picked up the call, and she said, Mr. Wesley, do you remember me? I said no! Then she said, " You helped me several years ago. You gave me money when I was stranded on a journey due to our vehicle breakdown. And she mentioned her name and the city where this incident happened several years ago when I was still in Africa. I remembered the day vividly. And said to her, "Were you the lady that was traveling to Lagos and did not have money?" She said, "Yes," and I said," We give God the glory that I was able to help."

Sometimes help can come from an unexpected person or from someone close to you or even a friend. Please never forget to keep a good relationship with such people. So please take this now as an assignment, pick up a pen, and think about your life from when you were young until now. And write out the names of those who have really helped you in a remarkable way. And try to look for them and call them. Just tell them, "I remember what you did for me so and so years ago and thought about you and decided to say thank you. Do this, and you would see how amazing it could be to show your appreciation afresh.

After you have done this, sit down and think again of the blessings of God in your life.

Remember to count them one by one, and it will surprise you how merciful God has been to you.

King David said, It is God who made you, and you are his. You are his people. The sheep of his pasture, you must continue to show gratitude. In all circumstances, be thankful to God. We need to be grateful at all times. If not for the need to be appreciative, but for our own good: Gratitude does a lot to the human body, soul, and spirit.

Gratitude blocks negative emotions. It reduces stress. Gratitude helps to eliminate envy, regrets, and resentment. Gratitude strengthens our social ties. It helps us to recognize what help we have received. It helps us to understand that we are all limited in capabilities. Only God has it all. Without gratitude, we are limiting our help. So let us show gratitude at all times. Count Your Blessings!

Chapter 11

DELAY IS NOT DENIAL.

Each time I think about Abraham in the Bible, it amazes me so much that it reminds me of the mysteriousness of God. Abraham was 75 years old when God called him and promised to make him a great nation. 24 years later, at 99, that promise had not been fulfilled. You can imagine the delay! Ok, let us look at Sarah, Abraham's wife. She was 65 years old when God promised to make her a mother, at an age when she was already too old to bear children. But then, God repeated His promise when she was 89 and fulfilled the promise to her when she was 90 years old and Abraham was 100 years old. How amazing!

This couple may have been praying for a child at a much younger age before.

Abraham's call: Perhaps for over 10 years or even 20 years, because his younger brothers already had children at a much younger age. So, imagine the wait. Today people are just too anxious for results. There is no patience in our world today. You pray for something today, and tomorrow you are already questioning God. God, why? What have I done to deserve this? Some people would begin to seek alternative means. They conclude that God is not answering them. Please, I want you to know that God's plan for you is a good plan. Therefore, never lose hope. Your delay is not a denial from God.

Abraham continued to believe and hope. He did not lose his confidence. He trusted God. He knew that if God said it, he would do it. Is there something you are believing God for? Have you been praying to God for something? Did you not get a response yet? Do not quit believing. Do not lose faith; trust in God, for your delay is not a denial.

Having faith is evidence of things hoped for without seeing them yet.

The question is, are you willing to wait for your answers? Will you wait for God's promise? Will you wait for God's answer?

I remember when I came to the US in 2015 for the first time and joined a community church in East Palo Alto, California. I was asked to preach on one of the Sundays. The church leadership was already aware that I was a minister. But the interim pastor objected to it, so they stopped me from preaching. I had already prepared my sermon and kept it in my files and believed that one day I would have the opportunity to preach the sermon. And it took more than six years of waiting before I finally had the opportunity to preach. I understood that God gave me the message and it would be preached one day. When you wait on the Lord, whatever He says He will do surely comes to pass, and it does not matter how long.

Abraham waited for over twenty-five years; his prayers were answered at 100 years; his wife Sarah was 90ars old, and they had a son together. Thus, truly God's promise was fulfilled. I can imagine how they danced, how they sang, and how they rejoiced when God put a smile on their faces. God will put a smile on your face in Jesus' name.

Now tell me. What are you believing God for? Is it a child? A partner? A Job? Good health, promotion, prosperity? Trust me, if you believe in God, it will come to pass.

Psalm 30:5 says in part that weeping may endure for a while, but joy comes in the morning.

Believe that your morning is now. It is time to dance! Get ready for celebrations. Wear your dancing shoes and celebrate your victory. You must start celebrating in faith before you see the manifestation. Make your request by faith.

Chapter 12

COMMITMENT IN CHRIST

The lifestyle of believers during the early stage of Christianity after the ascension of Christ is the best example for committed Christians. If you read the book of Acts, Chapter 2:42-47, you will see their lifestyle.

Acts 2:42-47:

42 They devoted themselves to the apostles' teaching and to fellowship, to the breaking of bread and to prayer. 43 Everyone was filled with awe at the many wonders and signs performed by the apostles. 44 All the believers were together and had everything in common. 45 They sold property and possessions to give to anyone who had need. 46

Every day they continued to meet together in the temple courts. They broke bread in their homes and ate together with glad and sincere hearts, 47 praising God and enjoying the favor of all the people. And the Lord added to their number daily those who were being saved.

The above passage in the Bible summarizes the nature and style of the early Christians, who were committed followers of Christ.

They were committed to 4 major principles:

1. Obey and follow the teachings of the apostles
2. Fellowship together in the word of God
3. The breaking of the bread together
4. Prayers

They were devoted to these four things, though it was very risky to do so at that time. They were fully committed irrespective of the danger that their commitment posed. Let us look at the meaning of commitment.

What is commitment?

The dictionary simply defines commitment as "the state or quality of being dedicated to a cause or activity."

Commitment is like someone making a decision in advance, not minding the circumstances or consequences.

Like a soldier signing up to go to war for his country! Imagine a military man leaving his wife, children, and family to go to a war. A war from which he may not return. He agrees to fight for his country and die for the cause. He signs a death warrant, as it were. That is what commitment is all about when it comes to commitment to the course of Christ.

Your heart, your spirit, and your soul are involved. You are 100% focused.

It is like saying, "I will honor Christ, whatever the pain and whatever the cost. I will obey God's word even though it is the hardest thing to do. That is the commitment that we are talking about.

That is what the early Christians did. They inconvenienced themselves to follow Jesus.

I remember when I was very young, we used to sing the first two stanzas of the lyrics by Lydia Walker:

I have decided to follow Jesus.

I have decided to follow Jesus, no turning back! No turning back!

That is what they did. Those early Christians! They were committed followers of Christ. And many of them were martyred in the course of their beliefs. Some were stoned to death, some crucified, and some beheaded. They stood their ground on what they believed and suffered with all pleasure for Christ.

For those of you who do not understand how difficult it was to follow Jesus at that time, let me give you a brief background.

Christianity originated with the ministry of Jesus Christ, who was a Jewish teacher. He was in mainstream Judaism. His coming was already announced by a great prophet of God called John the Baptist. John the Baptist said great things about Jesus as the Messiah. He baptized Jesus before he was killed by King Herod

Antipas around AD 30, about the same time Jesus began to preach. And his preaching was not loved by the Jewish leaders because he told them the truth to their face, and he called them hypocrites. Jesus preached about the kingdom of God by telling everyone to repent. He was hard and bold in His messages and said He stood His ground because He was carrying out the assignment given Him by His Father, the Almighty God, and He backed His messages with healing and diverse miracles. So, the leaders hated Him and sought to kill Him.

Many people believed Jesus and began to follow Him. So, those who followed Jesus were hated too and were persecuted and even killed.

After Jesus was crucified, great fear came among His followers, and they became scattered in different places, avoiding public places. However, they would not stop worshiping God. They continued in their belief and were spread all over Israel. So the early Christians were those who defiled Judaism and continued to follow the teachings of Jesus Christ.

And that was a dangerous mission. It took commitment to follow Jesus. They decided to do so at the cost of their lives.

This is what commitment is about. Commitment is dangerous! Commitment is boldness! Commitment is risky. Commitment is selfless.

That is why the Apostle Paul said, "For to me, to live is Christ, and to die is gain." Phil. 1:21

He understood the risk of living in Christ; that is why he said if he dies, it is even better because it means he would then be with Christ. It was commitment that made him say so.

How committed are you when it comes to Christ? How devoted are you? To what extent can you follow Him? Are you willing to sign your life out for Jesus? That is what commitment is about.

Esther said in the book of Esther 4:16, If I perish, I perish. It was commitment to the courses of the Jews that made her say so. She was willing to die for going against the law for the sake of her people. This is what commitment is about. How committed are you?

Do you go to church late? Do you pray every day?

Do you love your neighbor as yourself, for the sake of Christ?

Do you support your church? Do you evangelize? How bold are you?

Esther said,

"Go, gather together all the Jews who are in Susa, and fast for me. Do not eat or drink for three days, night or day. I and my attendants will fast as you do. When this is done, I will go to the king, even though it is against the law. And if I perish, I perish."

It is commitment that made Shadrach, Meshach, and Abednego reply to the king in Daniel 3:16-18:

We will not serve your gods or worship the image of gold you have set up. How committed are you?

16 Shadrach, Meshach, and Abednego replied to him, "King Nebuchadnezzar, we do not need to defend ourselves before you in this matter. 17 If we are thrown into the blazing furnace, the God we serve is able to deliver us from it, and he will delivers [a] from Your Majesty's hand. 18 But even if he does not, we want you to know, Your Majesty, that we will not serve your gods or worship the image of gold you have set up."

Commitment to Christ is not without reward. It is not without gain here in this world.

There is a great deal to benefit when you are committed to Christ.

The Bible recorded that everyone was filled with amazement at the many wonders and signs performed by thes, and all the believers were together and had everything in common. They enjoyed the favor of all the people. And the Lord added to their number daily those who were being saved. Commitment is a key to growth; it is a key to unity.

Today's Christianity is becoming too cold, too ordinary, and too weak.

Christianity grew to this extent by the resilience of our forefathers in Christ.

They were willing to die for the cause that they believed in. They were devoted. They stood up to persecution. They stood by the truth. They were focused on their vision, which is why it did not go extinct in the face of persecution. Every believer has the responsibility to preach Christ wherever they are, with boldness and commitment. We are supposed to be a signpost for Jesus! Be His voice! And be His foot soldiers! Hallelujah!

Chapter 13

THE ULTIMATE FATHER

Once a year, people in America and all over the world celebrate Father's Day. Without a doubt, a father's role is important to every child. Honestly, to be a father is not easy. We must strengthen our children, discipline them, and correct them to achieve the desired results, and sometimes, the children dislike us correcting them truthfully. You can see that men are at the receiving end when it comes to disciplining our children.

Every responsible parent aims to give the highest level of love to the children. A good father would go to any extent to support their children to be responsible, obedient, and respectful. A father corrects his children, protects his family, and provides for them. He is firm in telling them the truth and reprimanding them when they make mistakes. This could create some ill feelings in the eyes of the children. Some would say my dad does not love me. Or he is too wicked. My dad is too hostile. Fathers endure all these to make sure they train their children right. A true father is willing to forfeit his meals for his children and sacrifice his time and money for their happiness. He gives it all for their comfort. A true father would love his child no matter what their situation is. He would cover his shame and stand for the child. And this is worth a great celebration.

However, this is not the situation with some fathers. Some fathers do not know what fatherhood is all about. They know how to father a child but do not know how to take care of them. They move on from one woman to another all for the purpose of 'enjoying' themselves. They are not ready to take on their responsibilities. Every child deserves the love of a father, and to all fathers reading this book right now, I say congratulations for your good work. You shall reap the fruit of your labor. Amen!

However, the purpose of this chapter is to draw your attention to a Father who is the father of us all, whether old or young, whether male or female, and that is the Ancient of Days. The everlasting Father, who was, who is, and who is to come.

The one who is able to turn our weakness to strength! He is the one who gave us life. He is the one who gives hope, and He is the Almighty Father. He is the Father of all of us: the Father of the fatherless, the Father of the orphans, the Father who never gives up. He is the I am that I am, the King of kings, the Lord of lords, and the Ultimate Father.

Our Ultimate Father is the final level that can be in fatherhood. He is the perfect father. The one from whom all knowledge consists! He is the source of how to be a father. If you want to be a great father, you learn from Him. If you want to be a responsible father, you learn from Him. If you get confused about your children, go to Him. If you get confused about your abilities, go to Him. And he will tell you what to do.

There are four reasons the Almighty Father is the Ultimate Father:

First, there is His ultimate love. 1 John 4:7-9

7 Dear friends, let us love one another, for love comes from God. Everyone who loves has been born of God and knows God. 8 Whoever does not love does not know God, because God is love. 9 This is how God showed his love among us: He sent his one and only Son into the world that we might live through him.

That God gave up His Son to die for our sins is a true demonstration of love.

We are saved or redeemed today because Jesus died on the cross. We are assured of eternal life because of the crucifixion. His love is ultimate; it never dies. Even in our sins, the love remains intact.

If you read the Book of 1 John 3:1-2, it says clearly that God's love for us is so greatly lavished that He allowed us to be called children of God. And that is what we are! The reason that the world does not know us is that it did not know him. Every person who has given their life to Christ is a child of God and, therefore, has been redeemed from the wages of sin.

The second is His ultimate provisions available to all His children.

He is Jehovah Jireh... The great provider. Jireh—Yireh means God will provide. Deuteronomy 2:7

7 The Lord your God has blessed you in all the work of your hands. He has watched over your journey through this vast wilderness...

Philippians 4:19

19 And my God will meet all your needs according to the riches of his glory in Christ Jesus.

God's provision is complete in Christ through His death, burial, and resurrection.

The mysteries behind the redemption plan are to make available to all the original plan of God that was first given to Adam and Eve in the Garden of Eden. Christ's death substituted for every sinner the loss that came through Adam's sin. This therefore justified all who accept Jesus as their Lord and Savior, thereby guaranteeing a restoration of their birthrights as children of God. If you have obeyed this condition of acceptance and confession, you can access healing of the body, soul, and spirit in Christ Jesus. It is indeed a mystery that requires faith and belief. Trust me, I have tested it, and it works. All that is needed is determination and a walk of faith. Our

Father has made provisions already; all we need is to learn how to obtain from the well of abundance already provided.

The third reason is His ultimate protection.

Isaiah 41:10

So do not fear, for I am with you; do not be dismayed, for I am your God. I will strengthen you and help you;

I will uphold you with my righteous right hand.

He gives us ultimate protection. He promises to be with us in fire and even in the waters. He is the ultimate father. God's protection is eternal. He assured us not to be afraid, for He will be with us and strengthen us. He is ever present, and nobody can protect us more than the Father. He sees every arrow thrown by the devil and is always there to deflect the arrow. He made His word available for us to fight back at any adversities. All we need to do is study the word to understand what to do when troubles come our way. We are protected against death because our natural death will take us to eternal life with Him. This is the mystery of the gospel. When you understand this, boldness comes to you, never to give up in times of trouble, because you know it is only a phase of life.

The fourth is God's ultimate forgiveness. According to the Scriptures, God does not remember your sins after forgiving you; Isaiah 43:25, Hebrews 8:12. God's forgiveness is once and for all. That is why He blots it out completely, like it never existed. And this is one reason He is the Ultimate Father. When your sins are forgiven, you are justified and become righteous in His sight because Christ has taken your place. He sees Christ in you. Therefore, you take on the righteousness of Christ.

Anyone in sin today can receive forgiveness and eternal life in Christ by acknowledging their sins and asking for forgiveness from their heart. This process requires absolute sobriety and readiness to change. God sees the heart and knows when you mean your confession, and He is always faithful to forgive. You can be assured that He will not remember your sins anymore the moment you accept that Jesus died for your sins and promise to continue in that new life in Christ. You are also guaranteed a new start as a new creature in Christ. And as a redeemed person, you no longer walk as a sinner but as a believer, and the manual for living the life in Christ is the Bible.

So, when you are born again, you begin to learn how to live Christ's life from the word of God. All that we need to follow is written in the word of God, and to understand the teaching of the word, we need the Holy Spirit to guide us. Without the Holy Spirit, we may read the Bible literally and miss the interpretation of what God is telling us. Therefore, it is expedient to ask God for His Spirit to come into us as promised in the Book of Acts, Chapter 2. And the evidence of the presence of the Holy Spirit in us is speaking in tongues. However, it is also advised to get baptism of water in the name of the Father, Son, and Holy Ghost.

The Ultimate Father is the only hope for us to live life without regrets, with confidence, and with meaning. So, if you are not sure that God is your Father, this is an opportunity to make Him your Father. All you need to do is stand up, open your heart, and say the following:

"Father, I believe that Jesus Christ died for my sins. I accept Jesus as my Lord and Savior. I confess that I have been a sinner. Forgive me, Father! Have mercy upon my soul and write my name in the Book of Life, in Jesus' name! Amen!"

Congratulations! You are saved! All that you need to do now is to join any Bible-believing church and follow up to be baptized and filled with the Holy Ghost. Then, start to study your Bible; continue to participate in church activities and learn about God from your Bible.

Chapter 14

STEPS TO THE MOUNTAINTOP

In my previous chapter, I talked about planning as a principal step to take before embarking on a journey to success. And I defined planning as a step-by-step approach designed to fulfill a goal. There are different types of goals: career goals, personal life goals, organizational goals, spiritual goals, and so on and so forth.

In this chapter, spiritual formation will be my main focus. Spiritual maturity is the mountaintop for a Christian. Your height in spirituality as a Christian helps you to withstand the devices of the enemy, Satan. It is that position of growth that gives you confidence and absolute comfort in your belief and trust in God. At this stage, no matter the storms, you keep loving God because you know Him. You can now mount every situation like an eagle and fly beyond the mark of giving up. There is no more turning back because your hands are already on the plow. For clarity, this height of your growth in the word of God makes you a mature Christian.

Therefore, a step to the mountaintop is crucial for every Christian. But the question that comes to mind is, 'Who is a mature Christian?'

As for me, I agree that a mature Christian is a believer in Christ who has grown in grace and in the knowledge of God to that level where he or she is a partaker of the divine nature of Christ. This Christian demonstrates their maturity through the conduct they possess, including endurance, humility, and suffering, through Christ, who strengthens them. They are in conformity with the image and nature of Christ. That is, they are more like Christ.

When you are mature in Christ, your spiritual capacity is good enough to prevent the storms of life from blowing you away. You would have been filled enough with the knowledge of God to stand firm without fear. And you would have formed enough relationships with Christ to be able to navigate through trials and temptations that the devil throws at you.

For you to be at the mountaintop, you must have experienced enough in following Christ and gone through what I would call the 5 stages of spiritual formation. Those stages are salvation, discipleship, sanctification, empowerment, and fortification.

Salvation

Before commencing this growth process, you must first be a Christian. A Christian is an individual who is born again. This means the individual has given his or her life to Christ and accepted Him as His Lord and Savior. This is also called salvation. After you are saved, the journey of Christianity begins. This is when the individual is expected to start the training process. The training process includes being taught who God is and about the Son and the Holy

Spirit. You are then baptized by water immersion in the name of the Father, the Son, and the Holy Ghost.

After baptism, you are a baby Christian and need to be fed the word of God by a mature disciple who is already well-versed and filled with the Holy Ghost. Your training can take years for you to grow into the maturity needed to work as a disciple for other newborns.

Stages in Christian Growth

Baby Christian or Babe: 1 Cor. 3:1-4.

A baby Christian is one who is newly saved and begins to feed on the peripherals of knowledge as a Christian. You are fed with spiritual milk and do not have a deeper knowledge of the word.

Simply put, you do not yet understand the Bible. That Christian is still fleshy and worldly. So, you begin to learn what is expected of you to form the beliefs required for a Christian. This can take some years of consistent training and prayers to help you think, say, and do things rightly with your formed belief in the Lord. The Bible describes those Christians in 1 Peter **Like newborn babies, crave pure spiritual milk, so that by it you may grow up in your salvation.** When you drink this spiritual milk and allow it to enter you, you begin to form a belief that is difficult to break. And the signs are demonstrated in your behavior and ability to live your life within your knowledge of the word of God. You understand forgiveness, love, kindness, etc., exhibiting the fruit of the Spirit and avoiding works of the flesh, as listed in Galatians 5. The goal of the training you go through is to become stable in your ability to respond to the Spirit of God in you rather than your flesh. This is difficult because your flesh will fight back to retain control of you. It takes time to study and pray to achieve.

This process may take about four to seven years, according to Apostle Paul's missionary journey. It is hard to let go of the world and stop pleasing your flesh. It takes the work of the Holy Spirit to subject you to change. They are still heavily influenced by what they see other people do. They complain a lot and quarrel in the church. They are so easily offended in the

Church. They do not understand the love of Christ.

From being a baby Christian, you grow to become a child, or 'little children.' 1 John 2:1-2. 2: My dear children, I write this to you so you will not sin. But if anybody does sin, we have an advocate with the Father—Jesus Christ, the Righteous One. 2 He is the atoning sacrifice for our sins, and not only for ours but also for the sins of the whole world.

At this stage a Christian has outgrown malice, envy, and evil speaking. This Christian begins to crave more spiritual food. They become passionate about Jesus. They are eager to talk about Jesus, and they want to fellowship with other Christians. They may fall occasionally to the flesh but bounce back through hearty repentance.

They want to learn more. They want to know more about God. They want to serve. They want to share tracts or handbills. They want to invite people to church. Their desire is to know more about Jesus. They experience the infilling of the Holy Spirit. They may still be easily tempted because they may still be interested in worldly pleasures. People may backslide when they get serious temptation. However, their belief is already formed in the word of God, so they would bounce back.

The stage at which you retain what you have learned is when you put it into practice. You can still be tempted, but you are able to understand how to bounce back by asking God for forgiveness. Here, you begin to work in love of your brethren truly from within you, and you are able to forgive so easily. You do not fight your fellowship members or attack them. You do not lie about people, and you no longer fall into fleshy sins, like fornication or adultery. You are troubled when you are late to church. And you just want to be in the environment of learning about God. You have grown out of being a child. You are now a young Christian. Steady and ready to grow! Galatians 5:13. 13: You, my brothers and sisters, were called to be free. But do not use your freedom to indulge theh [a]; rather, serve one another humbly in love. You now understand what you are doing and are gradually cutting off from the influence of the world.

Stage 4.

Like a young adult, you are now maturing in Christianity. You are no longer carried away with the temptation of the devil: Titus 2:6, 1 John 2:13. You can easily forgive and pray for others. You are more concerned about the stability of others. You love your brethren passionately. You are now talking with a sound understanding of the Scriptures. And you are able to apply the Scriptures. You now know how the devil operates and would not easily give in to trials and storms. You love God more than anything. You are committed to the Church, and you are able to give to the Church and can support the Church in prayers. You can now be trusted with God's assignment. You are so passionate about church and church growth. You want to help others to grow too. You are sincere and sound in speech. You become a good example of a Christian, and you are not easily deceived. Here you understand God's given gift, and you are willing to use it for the growth of the Church. Though you are still young, you are now mature.

Stage 5

Fathers &s: 1 John 2. Here you are now, more mature. You are relied on to teach others, and you have probably chosen your part in church duties. You can lead other people to God, and you have enough knowledge to manage people. You could rebuke with love but would not put people down. You are able to work with anybody while exhibiting the love of Christ, and you are able to discern the devices of the devil. You can support the weak, edify others, and help them grow. You now begin to show strong characteristics of humility and grace. You are passionate about learning about God and want to know more of Him. You are devoted, and you exhibit the qualities of a servant of God. You understand trials and would have tasted the storms and suffering for being in Christ. You are bold and strong in your beliefs. You are a mature Christian.

Stage 6.

These I would refer to as a general: 1 Tim 5:17. This is a consolidation of the Fathers' stage. They are old and have been so committed to the word of God. They are very humble and want to help the Church to grow. They are experienced in Christian life. They have grown in their continuous training and are ready to serve even in their age. Some have been Christians for over 60 years. They are grown and are older ministers, deacons, and deaconesses.

This group has grown so much that they can teach pastors and deacons due to their spiritual experience. The Apostle Paul was one. They have so many mentees.

It is every Christian's goal to become a general: being quick to forgive, quick to discern, and full of wisdom. We all aspire to get to this stage in life where we can say, I have finished well.

Chapter 15

SALVATION IN CHRIST

I have talked about salvation in some of my previous chapters, and I am sure we all know what it is. Salvation is received by grace from God to partake in the inheritance of Christ. As joint heirs, we are ushered into a safety net as members of the family of God through Christ, who stood in the gap to set us free from the wages of sin. This is what salvation is all about.

But I thought there was a need to explain this further to understand our place in Christ and our expectations as children of God so we have sufficient knowledge of what salvation is about and appreciate the need to go out there to share the Good News.

Romans 10:9-10 gives a clearer picture of what it takes to be saved. The Bible says if you declare with your mouth that Jesus is Lord and believe in your heart that God raised him from the dead, you will be saved. This means that salvation is an act. It is an action thing. You have to believe and profess with your mouth. This means that your heart or your mind is fully involved in this process. It is not a lip service thing. It is practical from your within to your without. Your belief comes from inside of you. And your professing comes out of your mouth.

Salvation is more than what we see or think. There is another aspect of salvation that has to do with conviction. And this is not an ordinary process. It is supernatural. It is spiritual. The power of God is at work, and the Holy Spirit does the convincing. That is why it is sacred. I want you to understand this aspect of salvation so that you can easily apply what you learn to help other people. Anyone who believes in Him will never be put to shame because there is no difference between Jew and Gentile; this is what the Bible says. The same Lord is Lord of all and richly blesses all who call on him. It does not matter who calls on the name of the Lord; you get saved when you do so.

This implies that salvation is available to everyone. Whether you are a Jew or a Gentile, it does not matter. Whether you are white or Black, your color does not matter. Whether you are Indian or African or Chinese or American, it does not matter; your race. Your language does not matter. Everyone has the same access to His salvation.

Salvation makes Jesus your substitute. You are swapped with Christ when you become saved. Jesus simply stepped into your shoes and took your place. And the result is that God now sees Christ in you instead of seeing you in the world. You are no longer in the world but in Christ. It means that your relationship with God is restored. You can now access God freely. That is what salvation is about.

Somebody might say, How does this happen? So, let us look again at Romans 10:14-15: "How can they call on the one they have not believed in? And how can they believe in the one of whom they have not heard? And how can they hear without someone preaching to them? And how can anyone preach unless they are sent? As it is written, How beautiful are the feet of those who bring good news!"

Clearly this happens by hearing the word of God. And you hear the word of God when someone preaches to you. Somebody tells you the Good News, the good news of salvation. The question is, who preaches this word to you? Now the Bible says only the sent does the preaching. Now let me unfold the mystery behind this to you. God empowers someone to preach the gospel. That is someone anointed by the Holy Spirit. It is the anointing of God in you that makes your spoken word of God carry power (that is, Rema, Christo (the spoken anointed word)). It is the anointed word that does the convincing. There is power in the anointed word of God that comes out of the saint. When that anointed word hits you, it penetrates deep into your inner being to give you the conviction to believe. When you are convicted, you now believe in what you have heard, and the power enters you to cause a change. This change happens in your spirit being, making you another creature. From that moment, you are no longer of the world but a new creature in Christ.

That is why the Bible says that no one can preach unless they are sent. And for you to qualify to go out there to preach to others, you need to be full of the Holy Ghost, who empowers you with the anointing to do the work. He gives you boldness and gives you confidence to speak the word. That is why you must first be a staunch believer, full of Christ, before you can preach. To do this, you must feed on the anointed word to build your faith and become strong in Him who sent you.

Some people may ask if salvation is permanent. Well, to answer the question, salvation is received by grace. But to keep it, you must maintain it. After you receive salvation, your relationship with God is restored, and that relationship needs to be maintained. If you do not, you can lose it, because if you cut off the source of your supply, you run out of stock. As it is in the supply of electricity: If you are disconnected by any chance for not paying your bills, you will lose supply. When you were saved, a 'hose' was connected to you from God. So, if you cut the hose, you lose your supply; it is as simple as that. However, once you are saved, all that is required of you—if you fall out of grace—is to ask God for forgiveness and get back on track. In other words, if you happen to go astray or backslide after you received Christ, you can get back by asking God for forgiveness. Salvation is an opportunity for sinners to be saved by God's grace, which is made available by the sacrifice of Jesus on the cross. Accepting and confessing Jesus is the key. May God give you the grace to believe and accept to take a leap of faith without falling anymore, in Jesus' name. Amen!

Chapter 16

DO YOU BELIEVE?

Some time ago, I went on a personal prayer retreat somewhere around Menlo Park in California, USA. It was a wonderful moment to be by myself with the Lord for 3 days. At that time, the church that I attended was not too far from the retreat center, so I was in church every day to pray, following which I would sit in the sanctuary to meditate, waiting to hear from God on what direction He would be leading us as a church.

Some of my reflections were on sermons that I had preached in the church. I remembered I started on a Father's Day, where I preached about our Ultimate Father: how He provides for us, His children; how He protects us; how He leads us, guides us, and talks to us; and how He helps us faithfully. And I reflected also on the other sermons, like 'Delay is not denial,' how God's promises never go in vain, and the need for us to believe and trust in God for answered prayers. I also remembered the preaching on Commitment to Christ, where we were told about the early Christians and how they devoted themselves to fellowship together in Christ.

They were in one accord and enjoyed the favor of God even though they worshiped God in a dangerous situation due to persecution at that time. I also preached about faith: that it is the act of believing what we have not seen. We all know that faith precedes miracles. And without faith we cannot please God. It takes faith to become a Christian, and it takes faith to believe.

All these reflections could only show to me that God has a good plan for His Church. And it would take faith to believe and make it happen. But the question that continued to come to mind was, do the church members believe? Do they believe when Jesus said He would come for all believers to take us with Him to where He was going? Do they really believe? This question is for everyone who considers themselves Christians.

Do you believe that anything Jesus said He would do, He does?

Jesus promised all believers that He was going to prepare a place for us and would come back to take us. He promised to relocate us all to His Father's house. He assured us of enough mansions in His Father's house.

Jesus also promised that He would ask His Father and they would send the Holy Spirit to be with us. He assured us of more powers for more exploits. But the promise was for only those who would believe. And that assurance made by Jesus Christ was to His disciples, His followers, and, by inference, to all of us. He said if you believe in God and if you believe in me. The promise Christ made to every Christian is that they would be taken to stay with Him and His Father when He comes back. He also promised that He would send the Holy Spirit, who would teach them all things, and every believer would be able to do greater work than Jesus did. Those were some of the promises. And truly, as promised, on the day of Pentecost, the Holy Spirit came to indwell His followers. Today, many of us are living witnesses of the presence of the Holy Spirit in us as believers, and we have seen the power of God in action.

The question is, do you believe? Do you believe that you could heal the sick in His name? Do you believe you could do greater miracles than Jesus? Do you believe it?

This is the big question that we ought to answer. We must examine ourselves to know how much confidence we have in ourselves as Christians. If the Bible says we are joint heirs with Christ, do we believe it?

The challenges of today's Christianity are centered around their belief and their faith in themselves as children of God. I tell you the truth, there is no inferior Christian, whether you are Black, African, White, Tongan, Hispanic, etc. So long as you are a born-again Christian, you belong to one body of Christ; we are all children of God capable of doing more than what Jesus did on earth. But the question is, do we believe? Do we believe in our capabilities?

Belief is centered on faith, and faith is the ability to hold firm to what you have not seen, the ability to lay claim to what you do not have yet. This is what faith is about. Do you believe it?

Check your heart; ask yourself. Do you believe it? Are you ready to go? Look, there is no rocket science about this thing. It is not about us; it is not about what we know; it is not about what we can do. It is all about what is in us. Is it about the Christ in you? He that is in you is greater than he that is in the world.

Sometimes certain accomplishments look so unrealistic because of doubt. It feels unrealistic to some people, and they just faint. They do not think it is possible. So, they do not try their faith. Listen, you cannot please God without faith. The work of God is all about faith. I have tested it, and it worked for me. I cannot tell you how many times I have tasted the miracles of God. I am telling you what I know. Trust me! I have tested it, and the power of God is real. It is not in your intelligence; it is not in your beauty; it is not in your handsomeness. It is in your faith. It is in your belief.

Our God is a God of impossibilities. He specializes in doing what is not possible in a natural sense. That is why He is supernatural. And those of us who believe are supernatural. Our achievements are supposed to be supernatural. Please stop thinking naturally when it comes to what you want to achieve. If you are a child of God, you are a candidate for supernatural achievements. It is not by power nor by might; it is by the

Spirit, says the Lord. This is where Christians are failing every day. They tend to do things naturally. It would not work like that.

Romans 8:14:

14 For as many as are led by the Spirit of God, they are the sons of God.

Doubt has no room in the arena of faith. Those who doubt are bound to fail because doubt is the father of failures. Jesus' assurance is only for those who believe.

Thomas was uncertain; that was why he asked Jesus questions.

Lord, we do not know where you are going, and how can we know the way? He was not sure and might have been doubtful. Too many questions! But Jesus told him again, "I am the way, the truth, and the life. No one comes to the Father except through me. Oh, Thomas! Just believe.

Because of Thomas' doubt, he got a nickname: the doubting Thomas. There are so many doubting Thomases in the Christian world today. They do not understand the operations of the supernatural. They are just slow to act. They drag their feet. Do not doubt; believe! That is the key... Jesus said again, if you believe, anything you ask in my name, I will do. John 14:13.

Let us work with the Scriptures, and we shall see great results. Now look at the reason Jesus said our prayers will be answered: so that the Father may be glorified in the Son. It is written there in your Bible. So, it is not about us. But what about the glorification of God? The glory is His. He does it to glorify himself. Simple!

Every miracle happens to glorify God. All we need is to remove doubt and believe in Him and move with faith. He will do the rest. This is about your faith and your belief. It is as simple as that.

Ok, let me tell you what happened to me. One fateful day, I planned to stay at a homeless shelter in East Palo Alto for a couple of days while I did my prayers. But when I got there, the place was closed, so I told myself, "Let me go to the retreat center at Menlo Park" to see if I could stay there. When I got there, I was told that it was not

Possible, because they only allow groups for retreat in the center. I then requested to pray for some time in their garden before I would leave. They agreed, and I went to the garden to pray. While I was praying, I saw this Scripture: John 14:13:

13 And I will do whatever you ask in my name, so that the Father may be glorified in the Son.

So, I prayed a simple prayer. I said, "Father, I believe in you, and because your word says I can ask anything in your name, I ask you, Father, allow me to stay in this retreat center.

So I continued studying. In less than 5 minutes, a man rode on a bicycle to me and said, "Mr. Wesley, I was looking for you to tell you that I put a call through to the boss regarding your stay, and I secured a room for you." You can now stay by yourself. I was so stunned at how speedily God answered my prayer. After he left me, I shed tears of joy at the beauty of serving God. I knew God answered my prayers so speedily to glorify Himself. All glory goes to Him alone. There is nothing God cannot do. The question is, do you believe it?

I understand that it might not feel like it, but it does not have to feel like it; that is why it is supernatural. The abnormal is what happens in the arena of Christ. That is why we say He is a mysterious God. The feeding of over 5 thousand with 5 loaves and 2 fish was abnormal; the turning of water into wine at the marriage feast in Cana was abnormal; the crossing of the Red Sea by the Israelites was abnormal; the filling of the widow's jars with oil is abnormal; raising Lazarus from the dead is abnormal; Joseph's becoming a prime minister in a foreign land is abnormal; and Jesus' resurrection is abnormal. So you see that every work of God is abnormal; that is why He is a God of impossibilities. That is why we function in the spirit and worship Him in spirit. Everything about God is supernatural. So all we need to do is to function in the supernatural. All you need to do is believe and have faith. It is as simple as ABC.

There is no reason to doubt God after seeing His miraculous power in the lives of so many people in the Bible. And I am sure some of you would have witnessed His power in your life. I have witnessed it several times. I believe God can heal any sickness: He can restore any loss, and He can save anyone. The Lord said in the Bible, Come, all ye that are heavily laden, and I will give you rest. Please release yourself of the burden of doubt and believe that God is able. May God give all of you the courage to trust in God in the midst of uncertain circumstances. Amen!

Chapter 17

ACTIVATE YOUR
FAITH IN CHRIST

We already know that it is impossible to please God without faith. So, every Christian is expected to walk by faith in order to please God. However, using our faith in Christ to achieve so many desired goals has continued to prove abortive. This strain has continued to create a deep fear in putting our faith to use. And the question that always pops up within us is, What if nothing happens? What if what we speak by faith never happens, What if our expectation is not met?

These are some of the inner worries that make it very difficult to live by faith.

Faith is simply the act of believing that something that has not yet happened will happen, but trusting in God that it will happen in the name of Jesus Christ according to the Bible. Activating your faith in Christ is simply putting your faith to work. The woman with the issue of blood believed that if she touched the hem of Jesus' garment, she would be made whole; and she put that faith to practice and it happened as she believed. She may have heard about the works of Jesus Christ: How He went about healing people of diverse ailments and casting out demons from the possessed, and she built that faith within her that she can be set free if she encountered Jesus. She may have developed her faith with time from hearing about Jesus. She acted by faith and it worked. The question is would it work for everybody like that? The answer is No! Why? Because we all have different levels of confidence and belief. Our level of confidence is built from our experience and encounter with Christ. The word of God builds our faith and enables us to act on the word.

Our Bible which is the word of God has told us to use our faith to please God; so, we start from somewhere by testing our faith out. If you love God and you believe that God loves you, then you can build your faith by trying it out. Pray for someone who is sick. Lay your hands on the sick and speak by faith. Start with small things and grow to bigger things.

Before you start practicing your faith, you ought to do the prerequisite first. Faith is act based on your understanding of who you are and who God is. You must build your understanding of what benefits are available to you as a child of God. When you know who you are in Christ and who God is to you, you can find out God's will for you. This understanding takes time to get. It takes studying the word of God. You must hear and read and experience God's power to build faith. It is just like going to the Gym to build muscles with exercise; that is how you build faith by studying the word. But before you begin working on your faith, you must be sure that you have already genuinely given your life to Christ and have been born again. After these you begin to study the word of God. As you study and listen to sermons and pray, your confidence is built upward and your trust level increases; and you will begin to fill the power of God within you. At this point, you can start trying your faith out. There is nothing to be ashamed of here, even if your prayers are not answered instantly. All that you are doing is glorifying your God who has called you to worship Him. The power you are using is not for you. But because you are saved and a child of God, you qualify to use the power as a joint heir with Christ.

Romans 8:17; "Now if we are children, then we are heirs—heirs of God and co-heirs with Christ, if indeed we share in his sufferings in order that we may also share in his glory."

The power is from God and the faith is a gift also from God. So, nothing to be ashamed of or to be afraid of. Just give it a go. Imagine a child learning how to walk in the presence of his father. His father will look with keen interest and wish him well. The child may fall after one step or two a couple of times. But eventually starts to run. The child develops confidence as he continues to try to walk until he becomes very comfortable and then starts to run. So, it is with driving. Your confidence grows with time. If we know who we are as children of God, we study to make ourselves a good workman that needs not be ashamed. We then practice what we have learned. If the Bible says I can do all things if I have Christ, then it is true. But then I must believe it is true to practice it.

Whenever you come to request anything from God, you must do so with the conviction that you believe God can do it, and you believe it is His will to do it.

So many children of God have achieved great wonders by their faith. But the question today is how do you activate your faith in Christ? Can you do wonders? The answer is Yes; you can do wonders too. But how?

Well, it can be difficult for someone to believe in what he has not seen or what does not seem plausible, that is why you need to hear as many times as possible to build your faith on the word of God. We must believe that it is part of our benefit to receive from God after being born again. So, we have the right to function by faith being children of God.

We must also know that God's plan for us is a good plan; and that He has already made provisions for us to receive the benefits of Christ's death on the cross. Once you understand these truths you do not have to worry any more. All you need is to apply the following:

1. Study the word of God. Read slowly, attentively and repeatedly: 2 Tim 3:14-17
2. Pray and fast. Join a prayer group, etc.: Ephesians 6:18
3. Imitate Jesus Christ and other successful men of God: Ephesians 5:1-2, 1Cor 11:1, 1 John 2:6

4. Use your faith. Ask God for help to grow your faith. Do not rely on your senses: Proverbs 3:5-6, Isaiah 46:4, Matthew 11:28

5. Obey God's voice. Be bold and fearless. Do not doubt: Exodus 19:5-6, Exodus 28:1-14

Chapter 18

DOUBT—AN ENEMY OF FAITH

Some years ago, the Lord laid it in my heart to preach sermons on faith: I have preached about the wonders of faith and how to activate your faith. I am quite sure that we already know that faith is an action that we take because of our belief, and we also know that faith is activated by taking action. However, we ought to know that there are some hindrances to applying your faith to solve difficult problems or challenges. And one of those serious hindrances is "doubt." This is one thing that has continuously caused faith to fail in many people.

If you read the story in Matthew 14:22-33, you will find out that doubt played a major role in causing Peter to start sinking, while his faith made him walk on water. Doubt is the feeling of uncertainty or lack of conviction, and falling into doubt can change your confidence and persuasion in what you believed in. When there is a doubt about somebody, it means there is a lack of trust. And doubt can be about yourself or about others. It is usually a result of what you see, what you have heard, or what you feel. When there is a doubt, there is fear. And when there is fear, so many unwanted things occupy the mind.

If you read Matthew 14:22-33, you see how doubt led Peter to start sinking. He lost his focus on Jesus and began to see the boisterous wind and storms. Because of this error, his faith began to weaken, and doubt set in, and the result was him sinking. He had to cry for help from Jesus; otherwise, he would have drowned. He focused on his problems and began to lose sight of his Helper. This is what is going on in our world today.

People are easily diverted from Christ, from whom our help comes. Doubt is an enemy to faith.

And as Christians, our faith is anchored on hope and belief. We believe that there is nothing God cannot do. We also believe that as children of God, we have a right to His

Abundance: so, we build our faith and trust in Jesus, who is our Mediator. When we do this, God is pleased with us and grants us more grace to succeed. Faith is believing, confessing, and acting on your belief. You confess what you already thought of in your mind. And you act on what you already believed in your heart. God sees your inner self and acts on your faith.

However, doubt is unbelief confessed by your action. Doubt is the result of inadequate understanding of what God can do. When you focus more on the obstacle, there is a tendency of inability to process what God can do for you. And this can be very disastrous.

Doubt and faith arise from what you see, what you hear, and what you feel from within you. What you see determines how you feel or respond. When the disciples saw Jesus walking on the water, their first thought was that He was a ghost, and they were afraid. So, they cried out in fear. Jesus corrected them immediately by saying, "Take courage; it is I. Don't be afraid." That was when they saw Jesus differently and believed Him because they heard Him and saw Him. But then Peter, encouraged by the fact that his Lord was walking on the water, requested to do so and got approval from Jesus, and indeed he walked on the water. Yes, Peter walked on the water. His belief in Jesus gave him the courage to walk on water. He had no doubt at the beginning and walked on water.

But the moment he saw the wind blowing hard on him, his attention and focus changed, and he began to doubt himself. He forgot that he was only walking on the water because of Jesus, on whom he rested his focus. His walk was not by his power, but by the power of God. He saw something else and heard something else; that was why he began to sink.

So many people derail in life because of what they see and hear. Their attention is diverted to something destructive, and they are not able to discern the baiting and fall for it. If you are a believer, you ought to focus on Christ, whom you can always trust to direct your paths; otherwise, you can easily miss the way. especially when you listen to a wrong thought.

Child of God, what do you see? What do you hear? And who do you focus on? Whatever you hear determines what you believe.

The source of your belief is from within you. It is inside of you. What you hear in your mind is the real source. When you doubt or when you are not convinced your faith is weak, your heart is open to the devil, and your ear is open to the voice of the devil. And what he does is to speak fear into you. Speak falsehood into you, and the purpose is to make you doubt what God has laid in your heart. And when you doubt, fear and worry creep into your heart in style. And as you continue to think about your fear, you lose your confidence. The devil easily gains entrance to your ears through his antics of showing you the impossibilities of your situation. Doubt opens the door to your internal ear and weakens you. But when you listen to the Holy Spirit, your faith is lifted up and you become courageous and bold to take a faith step. Doubt is an enemy of faith.

Faith is a spirit; it has power. It is given to us by God because of our focus on Christ. When we focus on the word of God, we are strong in faith. When we pray, we are always strong in faith. But when we allow temptation to overwhelm us, we lose our focus and fall. That is why it is important to always study the Bible. Because it is a major source of our faith. You can also read books on faith to understand the mysteries of how it works. The work of faith is centered on your belief, and you must keep maintaining your knowledge about what God can do to build your faith.

However, when you lose faith and fall, you still get up and rebuild your faith in what you believe. That is what Peter did. Even though he doubted and denied Jesus, he still became a strong pillar in the leadership of the early church because he repented and built up again. He became so strong in faith that his shadow healed the sick. He was so bold in the early church days that the people marveled at his belief.

Doubt only shows to us that faith is a journey that takes time to build. So, when you doubt you are being human. It takes time to understand that we do not rely on our humanity for our faith to work, but on Christ, our solid rock. A lack of faith is simply a lack of adequate persuasion. It shows that you are not sure, but it does not mean you are bad. The devil only tries to discourage you so that you will not be encouraged to try again. Don't listen to the lies of the devil.

Doubt only means that you are not fully convinced yet. It only means that you need to do more work. Read more of the word of God. See the results of people of faith and improve your knowledge of who you are in Christ and the benefits available to you in Him. It is only telling you that your level of faith has not reached the place of your belief. Do not allow your doubt to scare you away. Do not allow your doubt to stop you from trying again. Do not stop saying it. Keep on speaking your faith in action, because God is not done with you yet. It is a process, and it takes time.

Chapter 19

ACTION YOUR VISION

Vision refers to the will and purpose of God being made known to us. Everyone should remember to ask God to open our eyes to see the invisible and to hear the inaudible. What I meant is for our hearts to receive new revelation from God. This is because I have always known, a long time ago, that there is more to what the ordinary eyes can see. Sight is a function of the eyes, but vision is a function of the mind. A true vision comprises foresight, insight, and oversight. That is always a revelation from heaven.

We get vision through revelation. And vision applies to different entities: it can be for individuals, organizations, nations, governments, parastatals, and so on. It can be for a short time or for a long time. Vision is a state of being able to see beyond where you are. It is the ability to think, plan, and imagine the future. And this is born out of divine wisdom; that is, wisdom that comes from God.

There is no great person or organization or nation or church today that did not act on a vision. Every success story is built out of a great vision. Habakkuk 2:2 clearly explains that the Lord wants us to write what we see in our revelation. We are also expected to run with it because it is a revelation from God; writing it means that you are takingng a leap of faith. When you run with God's revelation, it feels fulfilling because you feel the impact within you confirming your persuasion in what you heard or saw. You run with faith. You run like it has happened already.

You cannot run with a vision you do not understand or know. You must write it down; crest it in your heart before you run with it. This has to be real from within you.

Community, what is your vision? You cannot run with what you do not have, because the direction of your race is towards your vision. This is serious business! You have to be committed; you have to believe, and you have to run with it. When there is nothing to run with, you would have no direction, similar to a scalar quantity that has no direction.

If there is no vision, there are no eyes. The Bible records in Matthew 6:22 that our eyes are the lamp of the body. Proverbs 29:18 says, Where there is no vision, the people perish: but he that keepeth the law, happy is he.

PERISH in the Greek language is called APPOLUMI.

APPOLUMI means 'To Be Destroyer.' It also means 'to die,' 'to be consumed,' 'to lose,' and 'to be utterly wasted.' It is that strong! And we must understand that a lack of vision makes you static. So, you can understand how serious the need to run with a vision is. That is why the Lord said to Habakkuk to write it down and run with it. Your life depends on it, as it were. The idea is to engrave it in your heart and walk with it wherever you go, because the lack of it is death.

For example, my ministry to the homeless and the drug addicts was given to me during a prayer session some years ago, and I have never rested from it, because it feels fresh always, like I just heard God. It is so strong in my heart that I have never stopped running with it. All we need to do is to run with our vision and never relent in our efforts to see it come to pass.

As believers, our common vision is to bring people to Christ. There is no vision greater than this—the increase through soul-winning to populate the kingdom of God. What I do in my ministry is to help people with addiction problems and give them the knowledge that only God can heal them through the power of the Holy Ghost. I am depopulating the kingdom of the devil and bringing awareness of the source of truth to the lost.

No vision speaks at the beginning. Vision begins from scratch. It starts bottom-up: with one step at a time. Stay with your vision to the end. Vision may look stupid, but if you hang on there enough, you will see it come to pass. When you believe in God and understand His capabilities, it is easier to follow your vision because He gives you the strength to carry on. God means whatever He says, however stupid it may sound to you. Heaven and earth may pass away, but Jesus never fails.

If you hear from God, stay there. If you work by vision, things begin to work supernaturally. All you need is to start. All you need is to action your vision. Vision works inside you! And Vision walks with you; that is, if you believe in what you have heard and what you have seen. Just do what you are told. God never fails.

Do not drag your feet. It is not by might nor by power, but by the Spirit, says the Lord.

For the revelation awaits an appointed time; it speaks of the end and will not prove false. Though it lingers, wait for it. I remember the lyrics of the hymn by John H. Sammis.

"Trust and Obey":

When we walk with the Lord, in the light of his Word, what a glory he sheds on our way!

While we do his good will, he abides with us still and with all who will trust and obey.

Trust and obey, for there's no other way.

To be happy in Jesus, but to trust and obey.

Obedience is the key to activating your vision. The one who gave you the vision will provide the resource. Just believe! Obedience is the key to demonstrating your readiness. Take a leap of faith, and it will come to pass.

Chapter 20

DIVINE EMPOWERMENT

As a Christian, you are a new creature in Christ and a candidate for heaven. However, you would need to grow your spiritual strength in Christ through a series of training and prayers to grow your divine grace, which has been made available to you at salvation. As you grow in Christ, you will get to a level when the measure of your faith is enough to separate you from the world completely. This is what is known as sanctification. However, this growth continues for a lifetime.

Divine empowerment is an impartation of God's ability to achieve something that is ordinarily impossible to do. Such empowerment is a divine power given to a believer by the Holy Spirit. It enables you to carry out the assignment of God upon your life and helps you with inspiration to function. Every Christian shares in God's divine grace. But the measure of grace is determined by their measure of faith.

Heb. 11:1 states that faith is the substance of things hoped for and the evidence of things not seen; however, to obtain the impartation of power to operate in divine grace requires a certain level of trust. And this comes from how we walk with God.

For believers to start working in power, they must have developed their faith in Christ to a certain level by obedience to God's command. This is because empowerment comes with great responsibilities and commitment.

So, when a believer has faith in Christ, he is capable of achieving divine goals. Goals that he could not achieve ordinarily. However, your measure of faith in Christ determines the grace available to you for exploits. When a child of God continues to build his relationship with God through prayers and study of the word of God, he grows in faith and in the power of God. That is, the Holy Spirit begins to infill him and indwell him. This power in him is the Divine Empowerment of the Holy Spirit. This enables the believer to speak forth his blessings. It is just like saving money at the bank. As you pray and study the word of God, as you fast and pray, as you learn more and increase in your knowledge of God, your bank deposit in heaven increases and the power of God in you increases. This is the divine empowerment that quickens your spirit to do beyond the ordinary, because you can draw from your heavenly account here on earth.

You can use your divine deposit in this physical world. You can continue to build your faith with spiritual exercise.

In Luke 10, the Bible records that Jesus sent seventy disciples into the city to harvest souls. These believers were empowered and sent out for exploits. Jesus sent them out because they had received enough training in his knowledge and understanding to work by faith. They have increased in faith and divine grace. They have banked enough power in their heavenly account. They were ready for work; that is why He sent them without any money, food, or bags. They had enough of the grace of God. All that they needed was their faith to draw from their heavenly account. All that was needed was to speak the word.

They were already empowered by God to carry out their work. Jesus referred to them as lambs among wolves. This is because they were going to face dangerous and demonic people out there who would stop at nothing trying to devour them. They were innocent and harmless people, but they were fortified by the power of God. And Jesus assured them of God's presence with them.

Imagine the situation naturally! They would not survive ordinarily. Can a lamb survive a fight with a wolf? No! The wolf would devour a lamb. He will eat the lamb easily. But these people were already sanctified by Christ. They have been empowered by God, and they were more than conquerors. Ordinarily, they would not survive the demons, but they were different. They were carrying the nature of Christ. They trusted in the one who sent them; they believed, and they had faith. Therefore, demons succumbed to them. All that was needed was to have faith.

This is what divine empowerment is about: Ability given by God to his servants to do above and beyond normal. We are all supposed to be able to do big things for God. All we need is to build our faith, grow the grace of God in us, and believe. We have no need to fear. It is not by our power, it is not by our might, but by the spirit of God. Zechariah 4:6

It is God who empowers you to do anything for Him. He calls us, and He prepares us and sends us. That is how it works. We must understand that all power belongs to God. He is our Father and makes His power available to us to use. "God has not given us the spirit of fear, but of power and a sound mind": 2 Timothy 1:7

We can do all things through Christ, who strengthens us. Empowerment is a product of divine connection. And there is only one way to get connected to God: that is, through His Son, Jesus Christ. When you give your life to Jesus, as you receive Him as your Lord and as your Savior, it begins the journey of your link with divinity; and as you continue in faithfulness to Christ by obeying His command, there is a transformation that comes to you that separates you from the world unto Christ. This is what brings empowerment.

Empowerment is what helps you to do the unusual.

It helps you to forgive when you would not forgive ordinarily. It helps you believe when it does not look feasible.

It helps you to act without doubt.

It gives you peace in the midst of troubles or challenges.

It helps you to love those who even hate you.

Empowerment is the greatest asset for every Christian.

We are all entitled to it because it is a product of grace. But we must do something to earn it.

Do you want to do exploits for God? Do you want His empowerment? Do you want to speak to the demons and they flee? If you wish to function in the spirit, you can. All you need is to have Christ established in you. Then you follow the prescribed principles in the Bible.

Chapter 21

STAY IN HIS PRESENCE

Several years ago, I joined a prayer program organized in the church by a pastor in Thailand. And we were to pray all-night prayers twice a week. It was to last for months. So, we started every Tuesday and Thursday night. We would pray from 8pm to 3am. There were a lot of people involved, and prayers became so intense as we reached the 3rd week. And I remember it was about the fourth week that I experienced something that transformed my entire life. That fateful night, as I was praying with my eyes closed. Suddenly, my inner eyes opened, and I found myself in a different realm. I heard God's voice, loud and clear. He told me so many things I never knew about. He gave me revelations I could not have imagined. I was in shock because that was the first time I ever heard God speak to me. That program lasted for 3 months, and since then, my ears have opened to hear from God. We continued that prayer session for 3 months, and my experience changed my entire life forever. Ever since, I never would want to leave the presence of God, and I have never been the same person.

In His presence, you feel like you are in another world. A world of unimaginable ecstasy. It is so interesting that you would not want to leave. So, I can understand what happened to Mary while she sat at Jesus' feet and did not want to go: Luke 10:38-42. Nobody would like to leave that kind of environment of unexplainable pleasure. The presence of God sparks a new beginning in your life. The Bible says in 2 Cor 5:17:

17 Therefore, if anyone is in Christ, he is a new creation; old things have passed away; behold, all things have become new.

It is the newness in Christ that makes you look strange to the world. Martha saw the strangeness in Mary's behavior. To her, Mary should be helping out with the cooking. But she would not understand the peace and comfort the presence of God gave Mary. She was calm, relaxed, and concentrating. She was focused on Jesus and was not distracted by any other activities. When you focus on Jesus, you feel His presence. When you focus on His words, you receive knowledge because His presence makes known to you the mysterious things you never knew or heard of. That is who you become when you spend time with Jesus: You become a wonder to the world. Imagine how people felt when they saw the numerous miracles performed by Jesus' disciples.

Acts 4:13 states that when they saw the boldness of Peter and John and perceived that they were unlearned and ignorant men, they marveled, and they took knowledge of them, that they had been with Jesus.

Being with Christ has so many benefits that we cannot count them. Some of which are as follows:

In His presence there is liberty. 2 Corinthians 3:17: 17 Now the Lord is the Spirit, and where the Spirit of the Lord is, there is liberty.

In His presence there is joy: Psalm 16:11. The joy of the indwelling of the Holy Spirit is unexplainable.

In His presence there is peace: Ephesians 2:14-16: 14 For He Himself is our peace, who has made both one and has broken down the middle wall of separation, 15 having abolished in His flesh the enmity, that is, the law of commandments contained in ordinances, so as to create in Himself one new man from the two, thus making peace, 16 and that He might reconcile them both to God in one body through the cross, thereby putting to death the enmity.

In His presence there is knowledge. Proverbs 9:10: "The fear of the LORD is the beginning of wisdom, and the knowledge of the Holy One is understanding.

In His presence there is power: Matthew 28:18-20: 18 And Jesus came and spoke to them, saying, "All authority has been given to Me in heaven and on earth. 19 Go therefore and make disciples of all the nations, baptizing them in the name of the Father and of the Son and of the Holy Spirit, 20 teaching them to observe all things that I have commanded you; and lo, I am with you always, even to the end of the age.

Chapter 22

RESTORATION
FROM REPENTANCE

Some years ago, a guest minister in our church explained in his sermon that we are all in a war with invisible beings. This is true because the Bible states in Ephesians 6:12 that we wrestle not against flesh and blood, but against forces in high places. Forces of darkness are spiritual beings we can neither see nor touch nor fight physically. They are invisible and therefore cannot be fought with our physical fists. Spiritual battles are fought spiritually.

As human beings, we cannot fight invisible beings. We only rely on God to fight our battles for us because our God sees every plan of the wicked. We can see neither him nor his agents. Satan has a very organized network, and they have the capabilities of inhabiting human beings to manipulate them as their prey. That is why it is important for us as Christians to remain connected with our God for protection.

Spiritual battles do not need judo and karate skills or warplanes and guns; they need prayers. They need the application of the word of God. If you study the Bible, you will see how men of God fought those battles. And you can follow in their footsteps.

For example, Moses faced King Pharaoh in his palace to demand the release of the Israelites from slavery. David faced Goliath as a teenager; Elijah killed 450 prophets of Baal alone.

These great men of God fought their battles by faith in God Almighty. God fought their battles for them.

They fought impossible battles not by their power, but by the Spirit of God. They completely relied on God to succeed against their enemies.

2 Chronicles 20:15 says the battle is the Lord's, not yours!

Now tell me, if God is not with us, how can we fight our battles?

Many believers and churches are very vulnerable today because God is not present with them to fight their battles. Many people today are easy prey to their enemies because God is not with them. So many churches have become cold because the Holy Spirit has left them.

They are powerless; there are no signs and wonders following them, contrary to what is promised by God in Mark 16:17:

"And these signs will accompany those who believe: In my name they will drive out demons; they will speak in new tongues."

The Holy Spirit left them because of disobedience. The Holy Spirit left because of sins. God cannot behold sin. God cannot behold disobedience. We are all in the equity of these errors. We have all sinned and come short of the glory of God. It is a problem that needs to be fixed by the Church, by families, by couples, among brothers and sisters, and among brethren in the Church. It is a problem that must be solved.

The Bible says in Romans 6:2, Shall we continue in sins and expect grace to abound? God forbid!

Jesus said in Matthew 7:21-23 Not everyone that says, Lord, Lord, will enter the Kingdom of God.

This is because He saw the pretense of some Pharisees in the temple of God.

Some Christians live in their illusion that everything is ok. But God sees; He knows that everything is not okay. We cannot hide our sins from God. Stop pretending if you know that you are in error. Please! We cannot deceive God. Do not say everything is in God's hands. No! It is in our hands. Life with Christ does not work like that. We must take responsibility. We must acknowledge our disobedience to God and make restitution. We must beg for forgiveness. We must humble ourselves and acknowledge that we have sinned.

We need to do this; we cannot jump the gun. Do not be in a hurry. Do the needful now. Accept that you messed up and beg God for forgiveness.

That is what we must do before restoration can come. And restoration comes from repentance. No one is too big to ask God for forgiveness. Romans 3:23 says, All have sinned and come short of the glory of God. We can ask for forgiveness. Disobedience brings the wrath of God. It brings the judgment of God.

Our God is a jealous God. We may not be able to interpret all sins. The Bible describes all unrighteousness as sin.

You know, the judgment of God could be a mere correction: He could say, You do not do this or that again." He could make a simple rebuke, but it could also be a punishment, a warning, or a smack. Unrepentant sinners may be delivered to their enemies. And when this happens, the enemy takes possession and begins to control the sinner. The devil is moving about seeking whom to devour. So a sinner is open to captivity. This happened to the Israelites many times in the Bible. And they got back to freedom after they sobered up and begged God for forgiveness.

How do you know there is a serious problem? You know there is a problem when things start to fall apart, when there is an argument in a marriage every time, when there is frequent disagreement between married couples, between

leaders in churches, between brothers and sisters, between siblings, when there are killings in the society, immorality, sexual sins, infidelity, strife, among others. Yes, you consider that there is a serious problem when members are deserting, when there is difficult confusion, discouragement, weariness, or the like.

If you see any of these signs, please go down on your knees as a couple, as a family, as a church, as church leaders, or even as an individual, go down on your knees and ask God for forgiveness. God is the only source of our healing and our restoration; He alone can handle our battles.

The Bible says in 2 Chronicles 7:13-15:

"When I shut up the heavens so that there is no rain, or command locusts to devour the land, or send a plague among my people, if my people, who are called by my name, will humble themselves and pray and seek my face and turn from their wicked ways, then I will hear from heaven, and I will forgive their sin and will heal their land. Now my eyes will be open and my ears attentive to the prayers offered in this place."

This is the promise of God concerning those who repent of their sins: they shall be restored. God is always waiting for His people to acknowledge their sins and repent. Repentance is the only key to restoration.

You cannot repent without prayers. You cannot repent without acknowledging you have sinned. God is patient and takes time to wait for every sinner to ask for forgiveness. If we soberly repent, He will have mercy on us, cleanse us, and make us white as snow. God promised to open His eyes and His ears to the prayers offered. God is God. Whatever He says He will do, that is what He will do.

Chapter 23

DISCIPLESHIP

Discipleship could be viewed from different perspectives, depending on one's understanding and knowledge. The meaning is literally the same: the activities involved in helping others learn, with the intention of making them independent and capable of doing what has been taught to them. Discipleship could also be viewed from the Christian point of view, which is my focus in this chapter. Discipleship is simply the process of making a disciple of Christ.

We cannot talk about discipleship without understanding first who a disciple is. In my opinion, a disciple is a Christian, or a follower of Christ, who has forsaken himself to learn about Jesus Christ in order to be like Him. You cannot become a disciple without being a Christian, and you cannot become a Christian without being called. The process of calling a person to become a Christian is one type of discipleship known as 'preaching the gospel.' Telling people about the gospel of Christ leads to conversion, which in itself is a call from God. And the entire process includes a call to fish for people, to bring them to Jesus, and a call to fellowship with believers. All these processes are the very initial stage, or infant stage, in discipleship. And it forms the bases for a relationship with the lost, a relationship with God, and a relationship with other believers.

Discipleship impacts a Christian and empowers a Christian with the required knowledge and skills for demonstrating the humility and other characteristics and attributes of a mature Christian. According to

Matthew 28:19-20: Jesus Himself commanded His disciples to go make other disciples just as He had trained them. The idea around this great commission is to train faithful men who would in turn train others to follow the legacy of Christ's ministry on earth. And the goal is to reach all nations with the gospel. This great commission can only be realized through making disciples.

Discipleship, therefore, is the multiplication of foot soldiers for Christ, who are ready for battle and prepared for the great work of salvation on earth. And these foot soldiers must meet certain criteria in order to be called into this herculean task. Herculean, because of the responsibility that would be placed on them and the heavy burden they would carry as Christ's ambassadors. Matthew 20:27-28 and Philippians 2:6-8 clearly explain that the disciple must be willing to be a slave as Christ, who gave His life as ransom for many. To become a disciple, a Christian must be willing and ready for all it takes to follow Christ.

The process of making a disciple of Christ is in different stages. Here, I discuss three stages, namely:

The milk sucking, the meat-eating, and the bone cracking. When a disciple gets to the bone-cracking stage, he is deemed to be mature and capable of reproducing himself. I would briefly explain these stages below.

Milk-Sucking Discipleship: As I have explained before, the milk-sucking stage is the infant stage. This is the period of conversion and acceptance into the body of Christ. At this stage, an unbeliever gives his life to Christ and accepts Him as his Lord and Savior. He is then taught some basic Christian doctrines. And this would be followed by baptism in the name of the Father, the Son, and the Holy Ghost. After this, the person is deemed as being born again and a new creature in Christ (2 Cor. 5:17). The Christian will no longer live in sin; he begins to feed on the word of God. In the milk-sucking stage, the new convert is handled gently and tenderly as he begins to take the knowledge in like an infant would take in the mother's breast milk. And this takes some reasonable time before the individual begins to understand and work in line with the teachings. At this stage, discipleship has started and would continue to the next stage.

Meat-eating Stage: In the meat-eating stage, the beauty of Christianity is felt very strongly. The disciple would now begin to experience the impact of his new life. The stage is so wonderful because the person feels the awesome power of the Holy Spirit in him. He experiences the impact of the word of God in his life and the power of God at work. He can now chew the word of God. He could feel what I called the Pentecost experience in his life. That is the indwelling and the in-feeling of the Holy Spirit. He engages in solitary experience with Christ; he understands the divine purpose of Christ's death on the cross, and he can speak in tongues, cast the demons out of the possessed, and bind the foul spirits. He understands the Scriptures as he can hear, see, and feel the power of God in him. He now lives a transformed life in Christ, and his character and attitude begin to smell the sweet flavor of God. He is truly seen as different. He too can begin to taste a bit of the temptation associated with growth in Christ. And at this stage also some would have been given a special gift, an assignment by God. They would have understood the suffering and servant nature of Christ and been able to live a life of humility and willingness to follow Christ whether prayers are answered or not. This period can last years or a lifetime, depending on how committed and faithful the follower is. When the level of advancement or growth increases with time, higher challenges and long-suffering can begin to set in to propel the disciple into the level of discipleship called the Bone Cracking.

Bone Cracking Stage: Discipleship at the Bone Cracking Stage is the toughest point of Christianity. Just like I said, you are serving God because you love Him and you trust Him, not necessarily because of answered prayers. You are only interested in seeking God first, knowing that His plan is a greater plan. You now know that to die in Christ is gain. You now understand temptation as it comes, and you could only love God more in troubles. You are now able to teach others about Jesus. You are now willing to suffer for Christ. No fear and no worries. You rest only on God's divine promise. You are sober, sound in faith, in patience, in love, in courage, and in resilience. You feel the joy of Christ in you, even in times of sorrow and persecution. You are living in your calling without being dissuaded in any form. You can now replicate who you are in Christ in the lives of others. You are now a testimony.

Finally, we must note that in discipleship, the disciple continues to look unto those whom God would use to teach and train them as their leaders or fathers in the Lord and continues to learn new things even as the Holy Spirit leads us until we take on that immortal body as we meet Christ on that resurrection day. For example, Apostle Paul was a father to Timothy even until his death. Those who are called to ministry by God continue to walk with God in order to be able to work for God through a learning process that never ends, which is called discipleship.

Chapter 24

THE WONDERS OF FAITH

When we were growing up, we heard about the Wonders of the World, particularly the Seven Wonders of the World, and it was such a marvel that we asked, "Did it really happen?" How was this possible? But then, it is true because the sight of those wonders is still very much present today. For example, there is a statue in Rio de Janeiro, Brazil, called the Christ Redeemer statue. It is a statue of Jesus Christ constructed between 1927 and 1931. It is a massive structure of 98 feet standing on a mountain. It is so unbelievable in height and size that it was named one of the seven wonders of the world, being the largest sculpture ever in the world. Another example is the Great Pyramid in Egypt and the Benin moat from my hometown in Nigeria. These are wonders to behold.

However, there is something that is a much greater wonder than all the wonders of the world, and that is the wonder of the gift of FAITH. The Bible records in Mark 11:22-25 that if you have faith in God, you can speak to a mountain to be removed from one location to another location. There is no wonder in the world that is greater than that.

Mark 11:22-25:

22 "Have faith in God," Jesus answered. 23 "Truly I tell you, if anyone says to this mountain, 'Go, throw yourself into the sea,' and does not doubt in their heart but believes that what they say will happen, it will be done for them. 24 Therefore I tell you, whatever you ask for in prayer, believe that you have received it, and it will be yours. 25 And when you stand praying, if you hold anything against anyone, forgive them, so that your Father in heaven may forgive you your sins."

This is a wonder that is beyond human imagination. FAITH is an action taken to accomplish a goal. However, FAITH is of different degrees. With a measure of faith, you can achieve anything you ever wish for. Faith is a miraculous gift.

WHAT IS FAITH?

According to Heb. 11:1

11 Now faith is confidence in what we hope for and assurance about what we do not see

KJV translation says Faith is the substance of things hoped for, the evidence of things not seen.

FAITH is believing you have something which is not with you yet. You hope for something; you believe you have it and call for it by faith and it comes to pass. That is what faith is about: Believing what the word of God says and using your faith to get what the word promises all believers.

Jesus said: Have FAITH in God! And if you know who Jesus is, you will run with whatever He says; because Jesus is the Son of God and our Lord and Savior. Anything He says will never fall to the ground. Anyone who understands this concept and runs with it will never fail. The word of God is the key to all wonders. When you believe in the word of God, signs and wonders follow you: Mark 10:17-18.

Every believer who obeys God's instruction, always performs wonders. From the Old Testament to the New Testament, people who believed received and performed wonders. For example, Joshua believed that if they marched around the wall of Jericho seven times it would collapse. He obeyed God, believed God and took action; and the wall collapsed: Joshua 6:20.

20 When the trumpets sounded, the army shouted, and at the sound of the trumpet, when the men gave a loud shout, the wall collapsed; so, everyone charged straight in, and they took the city.

David, who was just a teenager, believed in God and he defeated a giant called Goliath the philistine, who threatened the Israelites in the battlefield. David killed Goliath with a sling and a stone. There was no use of armor and a shield. He was armed only with the word of God: 1Sam. 17:45-46:

45 Then said David to the Philistine, Thou comest to me with a sword, and with a spear, and with a shield: but I come to thee in the name of the LORD of hosts, the God of the armies of Israel, whom thou hast defied.

46 This day will the LORD deliver thee into mine hand; and I will smite thee, and take thine head from thee; and I will give the carcases of the host of the Philistines this day unto the fowls of the air, and to the wild beasts of the earth; that all the earth may know that there is a God in Israel.

David had FAITH and did a wonder! Something unimaginable! He single handedly killed a giant that his kinsmen could not dare to fight. David believed in the ability of God and used his faith. Anyone can do the same thing if they believe and have the same kind of FAITH in God,

John 11:40 says "if you believe you will see the glory of God". TRAIN your belief and start acting on it now.

Hebrews 11:6 says without faith you cannot please God. Belief is the key to your FAITH.

And faith activated is the greatest wonder to behold. And to use your faith, you must believe first on the word of God.

Romans 10:10 says

10 For it is with your heart that you believe and are justified, and it is with your mouth that you profess your faith and are saved.

Matthew 21:22:

22 If you believe, you will receive whatever you ask for in prayer."

I have prayed about so many things myself and saw it come to pass. I know because I have tried it and it worked for me. There is a Wonder to behold with your FAITH. FAITH can do all things.

Philippians 4:13:

13 I can do all this through him who gives me strength. You can if you believe.

Yes! It is true that your measure of faith determines your ability. Start from where you are and grow your FAITH.

Romans 10:17:

17 So then faith cometh by hearing, and hearing by the word of God.

Study the word of God. Listen to sermons and act on what you have received. You have to try it out: Use your FAITH. God honors His word. Take action. Say something. But remember to receive from God; your mind must be ready. You must have the right mind.

PRAY AND FAST. When you pray and fast you build power! You build Faith to open access to the Holy Spirit's provision in your life. And when the Holy Spirit enters a heart that is ready to receive Him, it gives unlimited access to heavenly supplies. There is A WONDER in FAITH

When there is no FAITH, the heart faints, fear creeps into your heart, and a fearful heart cannot take a leap of faith. This is the trouble with most Christians: They are afraid to dare If you trust God, take action. A lack of faith breeds doubts; and doubt brings so many questions. It is not the time for questioning. It is time to do something.

A lack of faith quenches your anointing. When there is no anointing, the spirit dies in you. When the batteries run out, whatever it powers goes off. That is similar to how faith functions in a believer. When a believer refuses to take the step of faith over any situation, he or she would not receive.

Remember the story of the woman with the issue of blood; she believed that if she touched the hem of Jesus' garments she would be healed. She did and got her healing.

Faith draws from the well of God's abundance. Every believer has access to God's abundance, but must develop enough faith to draw from this abundance.

Chapter 25

THE UNIVERSAL
LOVE OF GOD

Growing up as a young boy with my grandparents, there were over ten adults living in the same house with me. Most of them were my uncles and cousins. I was about the youngest.

My grandfather would force me to go to church with him. And he was very strict about this matter. And he would not relent to take me with him every morning when he goes to church.

I used the word 'force' because I did not ever want to go with him to church that early. He was a Roman Catholic and would only attend early morning service at 6:00am. He would call my name so loudly and yell, "Get up, let's go to churc'h. And he always did this when I was still wrapped up in my duvet enjoying my sleep. His shout would wake me up. Sometimes, I would struggle so hard to get up. And he would say, "As for me and my household, we will serve the Lord," quoting Joshua 15:24. It was pathetic.

I thought Grandpa was a pain in my butt because I did not like it at all. I never liked the idea of bringing me to church that early. But as time went by, I got used to it, as I would wake up by myself right on time to get ready for church before he came out to yell. I realized that what he did for me was an act of LOVE. Grandpa did not want me to be lost. He won me to Christ.

The reason I brought up this story is because there is something that I learned that stuck in my heart ever since I was young. And that is John 3:16: For God so loved the world that he gave his only begotten Son, that whosoever believeth in him should not perish but have everlasting life.

I later joined the catechism class to be baptized, and in that class two questions would come up almost every day…

Who made you? Why did God make you?

This question would receive the same answer every day until we all in the Catechism class turned the answer into a song.

Who made you? Answer God made me.

Why did God make you? God made me to know Him, to love Him, and to serve Him in this world and to be happy with Him forever in heaven. Amen!

Moreover, if you read through the creation story in Genesis 1 and 2, you would find out that the original purpose of the creation of man by God was to fellowship with him. That is why he created man in His own image. And He gave man the authority to dominate the earth and be in charge.

Genesis 2:15:

And the LORD God took the man and put him into the garden of Eden to dress it and to keep it. and Genesis 2:19-20:

19 And out of the ground the LORD God formed every beast of the field and every fowl of the air and brought them unto Adam to see what he would call them, and whatsoever Adam called every living creature, that was the name thereof. 20 And Adam gave names to all cattle, and to the fowl of the air, and to every beast of the field; but for Adam there was not found a helpmeet for him.

So, Adam was created to know God, serve God, and be happy with him forever. God did this out of His LOVE for Adam. He gave him the authority to be in charge of this world.

The Bible records that Adam gave names to every living creature that God made. Even the beast of the field and the fowl of the air. Adam was in charge. The CEO, Chief

Executive Officer. So, you can understand the LOVE that God had for Adam.

However, Adam disappointed God by selling out to the devil. He fell to the trick of the devil and sold his rights of authority. And that is the reason his generation would face a separation from God. Every human race: Whether you are White, Black, or Brown, all inherited this sin from Adam. That is why the Bible says, in Romans 3:23, For all have sinned, and come short of the glory of God."

The devil took the authority or the staff of office of the CEO from Adam because he disobeyed God. And Satan has claimed to hold that office in this world since then, even till now, using his position to terrorize the people of this world, to the extent that he boasted to God that his mission on earth is to roam to and fro seeking whom to destroy.

Job 1:7:

And the LORD said unto Satan, Whence comest thou? Then Satan answered the LORD and said, From going to and fro in the earth, and from walking up and down in it.

John 10:10:

The thief cometh not, but for to steal, and to kill, and to destroy: I am come that they might have life, and that they might have it more abundantly.

Satan's mission is to steal: to steal people's joy, cause pain, and steal people's peace. That is his mission in this world. Satan is a thief and a trickster. He stole the authority from Adam and has laid claim to it ever since, and he is using it to put fear in man, tricking men into disobeying God. He has continued to entice people to believe in his lies.

But God's love is so limitless that He gave His Son as a ransom to atone for Adam's errors. God made available an atonement to reconcile man to Himself. He gave His only Son as a sacrifice to mankind. And that is what this verse is talking about: John 3:16: For God so loved the world that he gave his only begotten son, that whosoever believeth in him should not perish, but have everlasting life.

God's love for us is so great that He does not want to lose His fellowship with us. That is why He sent Jesus to die for you and me. By this His original plan for Adam is fulfilled in Christ. The love of God has no limit. It is available to everyone in this world for grabs. Whoever wants it can have it. Jesus has given Himself up as a sacrifice for the remission of sin. He finished the assignment given to him by God the Father to redeem everybody from the bondage of sin. He did this through His death, burial, and resurrection. He confirmed it by saying it Himself while on the cross, that is, in His own words, It is finished.

John 19:30:

When Jesus therefore had received the vinegar, he said, It is finished," and he bowed his head and gave up the ghost.

Jesus affirmed that the job is done. And he again said that he has been given all authority. All power in heaven and on earth has been given to Him.

Matthew 28:18:

And Jesus came and spake unto them, saying, All power is given unto me in heaven and in earth.

142

Why did Jesus do this? Because of his love for us. His love is for everyone who believes. His love is universal. Salvation is available to all: to all who accept Him as Lord and Savior.

You can see very clearly that the purpose of creation has not been defeated. That same purpose is still very much available to those who believe. That same purpose of creation!

Still keep this formula in mind:

Question: Who made you? Answer: God made me.

Question: Why did God make you? Answer: God made me to know Him, to love Him, and to serve Him in this world and to be happy with Him forever in heaven.

www.ingramcontent.com/pod-product-compliance
Lightning Source LLC
LaVergne TN
LVHW051126080426
835510LV00018B/2253